THE ECONOMIC NATURALIST'S FIELD GUIDE

ROBERT H. FRANK

THE ECONOMIC NATURALIST'S FIELD GUIDE

COMMON SENSE PRINCIPLES FOR TROUBLED TIMES

A Member of the Perseus Books Group
New York

The articles on which a portion of this book is based originally appeared in the *New York Times*, *Washington Post*, *Philadelphia Inquirer*, *New York Times Magazine*, and *Worth* magazine, and to the extent they are reprinted here, they are reprinted with permission.

Published by Basic Books
A Member of the Perseus Books Group

Books published by Basic Books are available at special discounts for bulk purchases in the United States by corporations, institutions, and other organizations. For more information, please contact the Special Markets Department at the Perseus Books Group, 2300 Chestnut Street, Suite 200, Philadelphia, PA 19103, or call (800) 810-4145, ext. 5000, or e-mail special.markets@perseusbooks.com.

Typeset in 12 point Granjon

Library of Congress Cataloging-in-Publication Data

Frank, Robert H.
  The economic naturalist's field guide: common sense principles for troubled times
/ Robert H. Frank.
  p. cm.
  Includes index.
  ISBN: 978–0-465–01511-5 (alk. paper)
  1. Economics. 2. Economics—Psychological aspects. 3. Environmental policy—
Economic aspects. 4. Income distribution. 5. Finance I. Title.
  HB71.F6958 2009
  330—dc22   2008055536

10 9 8 7 6 5 4 3 2 1

Contents

	Introduction	*1*
1	Talking Back to Rush Limbaugh	9
2	Do Nice Guys Always Finish Last?	35
3	Money and Happiness	53
4	Trailblazers	69
5	The Dismal State of Economics Education	83
6	Thinking About Health Care	93
7	Getting Prices Right	111
8	Energy and the Environment	125
9	Winner-Take-All Markets	143
10	The Causes and Consequences of Growing Income Inequality	163
11	Borrowing, Saving, and Investing	193
12	The Economics of Information	215
	Index	*227*

Introduction

In an essay written in 1879, Francis Amasa Walker tried to explain "why economists tend to be in bad odor amongst real people." Walker, who went on to become the first president of the American Economic Association, argued that it was partly because economists disregard "the customs and beliefs that tie individuals to their occupations and locations and lead them to act in ways contrary to the predictions of economic theory."

More than a century later, the general public continues to regard economists with suspicion. My fellow economists often object that this attitude stems from the fact that our positions on many important public policy issues remain poorly understood. Although not the whole story, it's a fair point.

For example, economists commonly advocate auctioning rights to discharge atmospheric pollutants, leading critics to bemoan our willingness "to let rich firms pollute to their hearts' content." The statement betrays a comically naive understanding of the forces that guide corporate behavior.

Firms don't pollute because they take pleasure in fouling the air and water but because clean production processes cost more than dirty ones. Requiring firms to buy pollution permits gives them an incentive to adopt cleaner processes. To avoid buying expensive permits, firms that have access to relatively cheap, clean alternative production methods will be quick to adopt them. A firm will buy pollution permits only if it lacks such alternatives.

Auctioning pollution rights makes sense because it concentrates the burden of pollution reduction in the hands of those who can accomplish it at the lowest cost. It minimizes the total cost of achieving any given air quality target—an outcome that is clearly in the interest of all citizens, rich and poor alike. Evidence suggests that the more people learn about the auction method, the less likely they are to oppose it. For instance, although environmental groups once bitterly opposed pollution permit auctions, they now endorse them enthusiastically.

But misunderstandings of this sort are not the main reason that economists remain "in bad odor." There are at least three other important sources of skepticism about my fellow practitioners of the dismal science. One is that our traditional models of human behavior, which emphasize narrow self-interest, strike many as overly cynical. Self-interest is clearly an important human motive, but it isn't the only one. We vote in presidential elections, for example, even though voting entails costs and a single vote has never proved decisive. We leave tips in restaurants we will never visit again. Lost wallets are often returned to their owners with the cash intact. Focusing exclusively on self-interest, in addition to seeming mean-spirited, prevents us from saying anything interesting about an important aspect of human behavior.

A second source of skepticism is that economists' traditional models assume, against all evidence, that consumer decisions take place in social isolation. The plain fact is that evaluations of all types depend heavily on social context. For example, the same car that offered brisk acceleration in 1950 would seem sluggish to most drivers today. Similarly, the 3,000-square-foot house that seemed spacious to a corporate executive in 1980 would probably seem cramped today. And the right suit for an interview has always been one that compares favorably with those worn by other applicants for the same job.

Once we acknowledge that context shapes evaluation, many of my profession's most cherished propositions go out the window. Traditional models say, for example, that when rational people weigh decisions about how many hours to work each week and how much to spend on various goods, the resulting patterns tend to promote the interests of society as a whole. But that's not true when context matters.

Deciding how much to spend on a suit for an interview is a simple case in point. Experiments demonstrate that a job candidate who is better dressed than others is more likely to get a callback. This creates an obvious incentive to spend more on interview suits. Yet if all applicants tripled their expenditures on suits, the jobs would go to the same ones as before. Under the circumstances, it would be better if everyone spent less on suits and more on, say, preventative medicine and safer cars.

A third source of skepticism about economists is our traditional assumption that people are rational and dispassionate when choosing among various alternatives. Like the assumption that context doesn't matter, this one claims that socially benign results occur when people are free to transact with one another without restrictions. For instance, if someone with a poor credit history agrees to borrow $500 for two weeks from a payday lender at an annual interest rate of 1,000 percent, standard models insist that the state harms both the borrower and the lender if it prevents the transaction.

Since the beginning of recorded human history, however, most societies have seen fit to forbid loan contracts of this sort, ostensibly because people are not nearly as rational and dispassionate as traditional economic models assume. For instance, people often assign insufficient weight to costs and benefits that occur in the future. This makes the benefit of borrowing money seem misleadingly large in relation to the cost of having to repay it, suggesting a clear rationale for usury laws. These laws undoubtedly prevent at least some mutually beneficial transactions from taking place. Yet few societies have embraced economists' suggestion to eliminate them. In light of many people's inability to weigh current benefits against future costs, such bans don't seem mysterious.

In short, much of the widespread skepticism about advice dispensed by economists may be rooted in well-founded misgivings about the wisdom of the advice itself. If traditional economic models rest on inaccurate behavioral assumptions, why should advice predicated on those models be taken seriously?

Recent years have witnessed a revolution in how economists think about human behavior. The emerging field of behavioral economics devoted its earliest efforts to documenting the existence of anomalies that contradict the predictions of rational actor models. More recently, researchers in this field have introduced new models that better describe how people actually behave when confronted with economic choices. In these models, narrow self-interest is no longer the only important human motive, context shapes evaluation, and the consequences of systematic cognitive errors are explicitly taken into account.

Although these innovations have enabled behavioral economists to offer more realistic accounts of how people make economic choices, residual skepticism about economics continues to hamper our efforts to discuss these choices in public forums. Because the predictions made by our traditional models are often wrong, readers tend to discount our arguments even when the models are right. For example, when George Stephanopoulos of ABC News challenged Senator Hillary Clinton to name a single economist who favored her proposal to suspend the federal tax on gasoline in the summer of 2008, she defiantly responded, "I'm not going to put my lot in with economists!" Opinion polls suggested that the senator's decision to throw economists under the bus helped inflate her winning margins in the subsequent West Virginia and Kentucky primaries.

The insights of behavioral economics make it possible to discuss the economic choices we face in ways that don't insult the reader's intelligence. Since the late 1990s, I have been writing newspaper columns about such choices. Some have examined the economic decisions confronting policy makers in Washington. Others have considered the savings and investment decisions that flow through Wall Street. Still others have addressed the decisions we confront as individual consumers. This book is a collection of selected columns, most of which originally appeared in the *New York Times*, either on the op-ed page or in the business section. Although all of them were written prior to the inauguration of President Barack Obama, they speak directly to many of the political, financial, and personal decisions we'll confront in the years ahead.

Grouped thematically, the selections cover a broader spectrum of questions than many readers might expect to encounter in economics, ranging from why John F. Kennedy's "Ask not . . ." appeal was so effective to why people voluntarily disclose unfavorable information about themselves. If you accept my view that economics is all about choice in a context of scarcity, then virtually all choices are economic ones.

The behavioral economics revolution has done nothing to alter the fundamental economic problem implicit in every such choice: while human desires are boundless, the resources necessary to satisfy them are limited. We confront trade-offs at every turn; having more of one good thing always requires making do with less of others.

Failure to think through these trade-offs results in waste. Traditional economic discourse—as exemplified in the late Arthur Okun's 1975 book *Equity and Efficiency: The Big Tradeoff*—has conditioned us to think of efficiency and equality as competing goals. Consequently many believe that we must tolerate a certain measure of waste in the name of fairness. But I argue here for the opposite claim—that efficiency is always and everywhere the best way to promote equity.

In one sense, this claim is true by definition. After all, any step that makes the economic pie larger necessarily makes it possible for everyone to have a larger slice than before. Of course, there is no guarantee that everyone will automatically get a bigger slice. Redistribution is often necessary.

But efficiency and equity are often harmonious at a deeper level. Traditional economic discourse holds that while a more progressive tax system might be desirable on equity grounds, it would impoverish the nation by inhibiting effort and innovation. Recent developments in behavioral economics, however, suggest precisely the opposite effect. As I explain in my examination of the financial advice industry, for example, reducing the tax rates on top earners likely increased the number of aspiring hedge fund managers and reduced the number of aspiring teachers and engineers. Because we live in a world with too few qualified teachers and a huge surplus of people hoping to become money managers, these tax cuts have almost surely made the economic pie smaller.

In this and numerous other ways, recent developments in behavioral economics have rendered obsolete many of the long-standing disputes between traditional liberals and conservatives. As I argue in my discussion of John Kenneth Galbraith, when these developments support the traditional liberal position on an issue—as they often do—it is typically for different reasons. Liberals have long argued, for example, that safety regulation is needed to protect workers from exploitation by firms with market power. Yet as conservatives have consistently pointed out, such regulation typically has its greatest impact in the very labor markets that are most competitive by traditional measures. A more plausible account is that workers favor safety regulations for the same reason that hockey players favor rules requiring them to wear helmets.

As the Nobel laureate Thomas Schelling explained, hockey players gain a competitive edge by skating without helmets, perhaps because they are able to see and hear a little better. Yet when all players skate without helmets, each team's odds of winning remain the same as if all players wore them. And hence the attraction of helmet rules.

A similar logic explains the attraction of workplace safety rules. By accepting a riskier job, a worker can earn extra money to buy a house in a better school district. Yet when all workers accept riskier jobs, they succeed only in bidding up the prices of such houses. As before, half of all workers must send their children to bottom-half schools.

Once economic reasoning is untethered from the constraints of the narrowest rational actor models, it becomes clear why conventional ideology provides an essentially useless guide for the economic choices we face. These choices are always best made pragmatically—by carefully weighing the relevant costs and benefits of competing options. Thus in a choice between two mutually exclusive programs, the better choice is the one whose benefit outweighs its cost by the larger margin. Always.

Suppose, for example, that the choice is between two methods for reaching a given air quality target in Los Angeles. Program A would require all cars, new and old, to meet reasonably strict emissions standards. Program B would exempt cars more than fifteen years old from these standards but would require stricter standards for newer vehicles. Both programs would yield the same overall air quality, but because program B's stricter standards for new vehicles are costly, it is more expensive overall than program A.

The cost-benefit test identifies program A as the better option. But supporters of program B argue that despite its higher cost, it is still the better choice, since imposing the burden of meeting emissions standards on the mostly poor drivers who own older vehicles would be unacceptable.

As I explain in my discussion of this issue, however, this argument makes no sense. More than 80 percent of the smog in LA now comes from exempt older vehicles. The money saved by eliminating the exemption and adopting less strict standards for newer vehicles would have been more than enough to give every owner of an older vehicle a voucher sufficient to buy a compliant late-model used car.

Distributional objections are more difficult to address in some domains than in others. But it is almost always an error to regard them as insurmountable. Again, when a policy change makes the economic pie larger, it is always possible for everyone to get a larger slice than before. Astonishingly, however, many politicians continue to describe such policy changes as "politically unthinkable."

My grandest hope for this volume is that it will encourage you to join me in accusing these leaders of political malpractice. Waste makes fewer resources available to meet important human needs.

And since so many important human needs remain unmet, easily avoidable waste is inexcusable.

On a more modest scale, I hope to advance the pedagogical mission I launched in my 2007 book, *The Economic Naturalist*, arguing that a relatively small handful of basic principles do most of the heavy lifting in economics. Mastery of these principles is enormously helpful in dealing with the many difficult decisions that life serves up. Unfortunately, however, introductory economics courses generally leave no measurable trace on the students who take them. When they are tested on basic economic principles six months after taking one of these courses, they score no better, on average, than others who never took the course at all.

This dismal performance, I believe, stems largely from the fact that most professors try to teach their students too much. When students are peppered with literally hundreds of terms and concepts, many of them couched in gratuitous mathematical formalism, everything tends to go by in a blur.

The good news is that the most important economic principles can be mastered with little difficulty by applying them repeatedly to interesting questions from familiar contexts. That's what I've attempted to do in the columns selected for this book. As learning theorists remind us, the key to mastering new concepts is repetition. So much information bombards us each day that our brains have evolved this simple rule of thumb for avoiding overload: if you see a new piece of information only once, ignore it; but if it recurs frequently, develop new circuits for dealing with it. Since I draw on the same handful of economic principles to answer a broad range of questions, you will see the same arguments deployed repeatedly. If the prospect of learning to apply these arguments appeals to you, I hope you'll view this repetition as a feature, not a bug, of this volume.

Even if my reasoning doesn't persuade you to oppose waste in all its forms, I'm confident you'll master that distinctive mind-set known as "thinking like an economist."

1

Talking Back to Rush Limbaugh

In the long run, governments, like individuals and families, must live within their means. Although Republicans used to take pride in championing fiscal discipline, the national debt exploded on their watch. This resulted partly from rapid increases in government spending, but mostly it was a consequence of large tax reductions concentrated on the wealthiest families.

There are essentially two ways to reduce the federal deficit—cut government spending or raise revenue. Every presidential candidate since Harry Truman has campaigned on a promise to reduce government waste, and some presidents have made energetic attempts to do so. But not one ever managed to halt the upward march of federal spending. Deficit reduction has occurred only when the amount collected in taxes has increased.

Because no one likes to pay taxes, proposals to raise them rarely generate praise. So I've learned to anticipate a flood of angry emails whenever I write a column about the government's need to raise additional revenue.

The day after one such column appeared, I started getting messages from students saying that Rush Limbaugh was attacking me on his show. I don't have a radio in my office, but that evening I listened to Limbaugh's remarks on his website. No surprise. He merely reprised his familiar "It's your money" argument—people have a moral right to spend their pretax income in whatever way they please:

> It's none of your business, Mr. Frank, what people do with the money they earn. It's not your business to judge it. It certainly isn't your business to start making tax policy and economic policy based on it. But that's who the educated among us are, folks. These are the smart people, these are the learned ones. They know better than you and I.

It's easy to see why variants of this argument have long been among the most effective arrows in the right-wing rhetorical quiver. Because most people work hard for their money, they feel resentful when government takes some of it away. Yet consider the absurdity of the claim that we have a right to spend every nickel of our pretax income. If taxes were purely voluntary, our government would not be able to raise revenue to build roads or schools. It could not field an army, and if we were invaded by some other country, we would end up paying compulsory taxes to that government.

Perhaps those who oppose compulsory taxation should just move to a country where taxes are voluntary. But there is no such country. Given that reality, our best option is to have an intelligent conversation about what services we want government to provide and who should be taxed to pay for them.

THE columns selected for this chapter dissect the objections of those who, like Limbaugh, want to shut down that conversation. The first selection, written as the Bush administration was pressing for additional tax breaks for top earners in the fall of 2005, points out that although the earlier Bush tax cuts produced no real gains for their wealthy beneficiaries, the spending changes made necessary by those same cuts imposed significant costs on them.

1. Did the Bush Tax Cuts Actually Help the Rich?

When market forces cause income inequality to grow, public policy in most countries tends to push in the opposite direction. In the United States, however, we enact tax cuts for the wealthy and cut public services for the needy. Cynics explain this curious inversion by saying that the wealthy have captured the political process in Washington and are exploiting it to their own advantage.

Yet a careful reading of the evidence suggests that even the wealthy have been made worse off, on balance, by recent tax cuts. The private benefits of these cuts have been much smaller and their indirect costs much larger than many recipients appear to have anticipated.

On the benefit side, tax cuts have led the wealthy to buy larger houses, in the seemingly plausible expectation that doing so will make them happier. As economists increasingly recognize, however, well-being depends less on how much people consume in absolute terms than on the social context in which consumption occurs. Compelling evidence suggests that, for the wealthy in particular, when everyone has a larger house, the primary effect is merely to redefine what qualifies as an acceptable dwelling.

So, although the recent tax cuts have enabled the wealthy to buy more and bigger things, these purchases appear to have had little impact. As the economist Richard Layard has written, "In a poor country, a man proves to his wife that he loves her by giving her a rose, but in a rich country, he must give a dozen roses."

On the cost side of the ledger, the federal budget deficits created by the recent tax cuts have had serious consequences, even for the wealthy. These deficits will exceed $300 billion for each of the next six years, according to projections by the nonpartisan Congressional Budget Office. The most widely reported consequences of the deficits have been cuts in government programs that serve the nation's poorest families. And since the wealthy are well represented in our political system, their favored programs may seem safe from the budget ax. Wealthy families have further insulated themselves by living in gated communities and sending their children to private schools. Yet such steps go only so far.

For example, deficits have led to cuts in federal financing for basic scientific research, even as the U.S. share of global patents granted continues to decline. Such cuts threaten the very basis of our long-term economic prosperity. As Senator Pete Domenici, Republican of New Mexico, has said, "We thought we'd keep the high-end jobs, and others would take the low-end jobs. We're now on track to a second-rate economy and a second-rate country."

Large deficits also threaten our public health. Thus, despite the increasing threat from microorganisms like *E. coli* 0157, the government inspects beef processing plants at only a quarter the rate it did in the early 1980s. Poor people have died from eating contaminated beef but so have rich people.

Citing revenue shortfalls, the nation postpones street and highway maintenance, even though that means spending two to five times as much on repairs in the long run. In the short run, bad roads cause thousands of accidents each year, many of them fatal. Poor people die in these accidents but so do rich people. When a pothole destroys a tire and wheel, replacements cost $63 for a Ford Escort but $1,569 for a Porsche 911.

Deficits have also compromised the nation's security. In 2004, for example, the Bush administration reduced financing for the Energy Department's program to secure loosely guarded nuclear stockpiles in the former Soviet Union by 8 percent. Sam Nunn, the former United States senator, now heads a private foundation that raises money to expedite this effort. And despite the rational fear that terrorists may try to detonate a nuclear bomb in an American city, most cargo containers continue to enter the nation's ports without inspection.

Large federal budget deficits and low household savings rates have forced our government to borrow more than $650 billion each year, primarily from China, Japan, and South Korea. These loans must be repaid in full, with interest. The resulting financial burden, plus the risks associated with increased international monetary instability, fall disproportionately on the rich.

At the president's behest, Congress has enacted tax cuts that will result in some $2 trillion in revenue losses by 2010. According to one recent estimate, 52.5 percent of these cuts will have gone to the top 5 percent of earners by the time the enabling legislation is fully phased in. Republicans in Congress are now calling for an additional $69 billion in tax cuts aimed largely at high-income families.

With the economy already at full employment, no one pretends these cuts are needed to stimulate spending. Nor is there any evidence that further cuts would summon outpourings of additional effort and risk taking. Nor, finally, does anyone deny that further cuts would increase the already high costs associated with larger federal budget deficits.

Moralists often urge the wealthy to imagine how easily their lives could have turned out differently, to adopt a more forgiving posture toward those less prosperous. But top earners might also wish to consider evidence that their own families would have been better off, in purely practical terms, had it not been for the tax cuts of recent years.

New York Times, November 24, 2005

GOVERNMENT bashers have also advanced their cause by citing vivid examples of wasteful public spending, ranging from the Pentagon's $600 toilet seat to Alaska's $250 million bridge to nowhere. The next selection concedes the point but then goes on to argue that even greater waste pervades the private sector.

2. Is Government the Only Wasteful Spender?

With President Bush's proposed tax cuts for top earners struggling to get political traction in early 2001, Representative Tom Osborne, Republican of Nebraska, rose to defend the White House.

"The bottom line is that it's your money," he said, "and you know how to spend it much better than anyone in Washington, D.C."

In the years since, variations of this statement by the president and other government officials have kept opponents of high-end tax cuts consistently on the defensive.

This talk has been effective in part because it appeals to common sense. After all, people have an obvious incentive to exercise care when spending their own hard-earned dollars. Why would a faceless bureaucrat in Washington, who is spending someone else's money, be nearly as careful?

The "it's your money" line is also buttressed by widely reported examples of government paying far more than necessary to get a job done. Famously, the Pentagon once spent $640 for a single toilet seat and on another occasion paid $435 for an ordinary claw hammer.

But paying more than the market rate is just one form of wasteful spending. Another is paying a fair price for something that serves little purpose. This second form of waste is more common in private spending, and is made even worse as the chief beneficiaries of the tax cuts race to outdo one another.

A case in point is deciding how much to spend on a wristwatch. Scores of full-page ads in December issues of the *New York Times* have displayed handsome watches costing several thousand dollars apiece and more.

The most coveted among them are elaborate mechanical marvels with multiple "complications," special features that enhance their accuracy. The tourbillion movement, for example, is essentially a small gyroscope that rotates the main mechanism about once a minute, reducing errors caused by the earth's gravitational field. The Grande Complication, by Jean Dunand, sells for more than $700,000, but lesser entries by Patek Philippe, Rolex, and other manufacturers can be had for $5,000 to $100,000.

Unlike toilet seats and claw hammers, these watches are costly to produce, so buyers who pay high prices for them are not being ripped off. In another sense, however, their dollars go largely for naught. For despite their mechanical wizardry, these watches are not as accurate as a battery-powered $30 Timex, whose quartz crystal mechanism is unaffected by gravity.

Then why do people buy the expensive mechanical watches? Edward Faber of the Aaron Faber Gallery in Manhattan recently described buyers of these watches as thirty- to fifty-year-old men who want "this 'power tool,' this instrument on their wrist that distinguishes them from the pack." A watch that fits this description must sell for more than the watches worn by members of the pack. So when the pack spends more, the price of distinguishing oneself also rises. And in the end, no one gains any more distinction than if all had spent less.

Other forms of high-end private spending are driven by similar forces. To celebrate Amber Ridinger's thirteenth birthday, for example, her parents bought her a $27,000 Dolce & Gabbana gown and hired JaRule, Ashanti, and other popular entertainers to provide live music at her party in Miami.

David H. Brooks, the chief executive of a company that supplies body armor to the American military in Iraq, invited 150 of his daughter's friends to the Rainbow Room atop Rockefeller Center in Manhattan, where they were serenaded by 50 Cent, Don Henley, Stevie Nicks, and other luminaries during a birthday party reported to have cost $10 million.

Although these events prompted much finger wagging by social critics, the parents involved did not behave abnormally—they merely spent their own money to provide a special occasion for their daughter.

For a party to be special, however, it must somehow stand out from other parties that define the norm, and expensive birthday parties have become a growth industry.

Kevin and Danya Mondell, founders of Oogles-n-Googles, a company described as an over-the-top event planner for children's parties, recently announced their intention to license Oogles-n-Googles franchises. Yet no matter how much parents spend, the number of parties that achieve special status will be no greater than when everyone spent much less.

On balance, then, there is little reason to expect large tax cuts for wealthy families to result in a more efficient allocation of our nation's scarce resources.

For one thing, not all of the dollars used to finance these tax cuts would have been spent wastefully by government. Most of the money recently cut from the food stamp program, for example, would have been spent by poor families to buy food at fair market prices. And even though government does buy some items at inflated prices (body armor whose price includes a profit margin large enough to finance a $10 million birthday party?), many of these items serve vital purposes.

In contrast, most of the tax cuts financed by recent budget cuts will go to families that already have everything they reasonably need. This money will be deployed in the quest for "something special." Yet because special is an elastic concept, the number of families that succeed in this quest will be little different from before.

New York Times, December 22, 2005

A COROLLARY of the it's-your-money argument is that the government should never redistribute income from rich to poor. If we followed this admonition, which no government does, the lives of the poor would clearly become more difficult. What is perhaps more surprising, however, is that prohibiting redistribution often makes the wealthy themselves poorer. In the following selection, I explain why.

3. How Do Antigovernment Crusaders Make Us Poorer?

When asked to identify the two most important items from their list of ten public policy commandments, most antigovernment crusaders pick (1) public spending shall be kept to an absolute minimum and (2) the state shall not transfer income from rich to poor.

No government heeds these admonitions in any literal sense. Yet they have had a profound impact on public policy decisions, especially in the United States. Often, however, their impact has been the opposite of what antigovernment crusaders intended.

The problem is that many compellingly advantageous public policies cannot be enacted without violating the two commandments. Every significant policy change benefits some people and harms others. If the gains to winners substantially outweigh the costs to losers, solutions can always be found that allow everyone to come out ahead. But those solutions often involve higher taxes and income transfers to the poor.

Regulations that limit auto emissions are an example. Because these regulations increase car prices, legislators in most jurisdictions exempt older vehicles to avoid imposing unacceptable costs on the mostly low-income motorists who drive them. Yet the cost to society of this exemption far outweighs its benefit for the poor.

For example, although fewer than 10 percent of the vehicles in Los Angeles are more than fifteen years old, these cars account for more than half the smog. Exempting the old cars thus necessitates much stricter regulations for new ones. But the cheapest ways of reducing emissions from new cars have long since been adopted. According to a RAND Corporation study, meeting air quality targets by further tightening new-car standards is several times as costly as meeting those targets by eliminating the exemption for older vehicles.

By raising taxes on high-income motorists, the government could finance vouchers that would enable low-income motorists to scrap their older vehicles in favor of cleaner used cars of more recent vintage.

The required taxes would be much smaller than the resulting savings from not having to adopt such costly standards for new vehicles. Both rich and poor motorists would win.

The problem is that taking these steps would violate the two commandments. Antigovernment crusaders have prevailed for now. The ostensible champions of economic efficiency, they have kept government budgets smaller and blocked some transfers to low-income families. In the process, however, they have made everyone poorer.

Some believe that minimal government is synonymous with economic efficiency. But it is not. As the emissions example illustrates, economic efficiency sometimes requires that government play a larger role.

This instance is part of a broader pattern. In health care, for example, the private insurance system employed in the United States delivers worse outcomes at substantially higher cost than the single-payer system employed in virtually every other industrial country. But switching to the single-payer system would require higher taxes and increased benefits for low-income citizens, steps that would violate the two commandments. So for now, we remain saddled with a system that everyone agrees is dysfunctional.

In the realm of antipoverty policy, most economists agree that raising the earned income tax credit would be the most efficient way of increasing the living standard of the working poor. Under this program, general tax revenues support income subsidies to those whose earnings fall below a given threshold. Its compelling advantage is that unlike a higher minimum wage, it does not discourage hiring. But raising taxes to increase the earned income tax credit would violate the two commandments.

Because the most efficient antipoverty policy is deemed politically unfeasible, many economists support current legislative proposals to raise the minimum wage for the first time in a decade. If this legislation passes, antigovernment crusaders will be able to claim, truthfully, to have prevented an increase in the federal budget. But they will have won a hollow victory. For unlike an increase in the earned income tax credit, an increase in the minimum wage not only limits job creation for the least skilled workers but also raises the price of goods they produce. Overall, it would have been cheaper to raise the earned income tax credit.

Antigovernment crusaders have also prevented the adoption of energy policies that would produce better outcomes for all. For example, economists of all political stripes have argued that a stiff tax on gasoline would relieve traffic congestion, reduce greenhouse gases, accelerate the development of energy-saving technologies, and reduce dependence on foreign oil. But it would also impose significant economic hardship on low-income families, making it necessary to increase transfer payments to those families. Both the tax on gasoline and the transfers to low-income families would be clear violations of the two commandments. And so gasoline taxes continue to be far lower in the United States than in other industrial countries.

That democratic forces limit the economic hardship government can impose on low-income families is a good thing. But sometimes imposing hardships on those families would create far larger gains for society as a whole. In such cases, we can always devise solutions that make everyone better off. But it is impossible to put these solutions into practice without violating the two commandments.

Is it better to solve a problem by spending two extra dollars in the private sector than by spending one additional dollar in the public sector? The two commandments insist, preposterously, that it is.

Economic efficiency is a worthy goal because when the economic pie grows larger, everyone can have a larger slice than before. Antigovernment crusaders deserve credit for emphasizing the importance of this goal. But as events of recent years have repeatedly demonstrated, they are often the biggest obstacles to its achievement.

New York Times, March 15, 2007

ANOTHER favorite argument by right-wing commentators is that tax cuts for the wealthy, many of which go to small business owners, are useful because they stimulate job creation. George W. Bush made this argument in defense of high-end rate cuts during both terms in office, and John McCain used it repeatedly on the 2008 campaign trail. While most new jobs are indeed created by small businesses, this argument flies in the face of elementary economic principles. As I argue in the following selection, whether a business owner decides to hire a worker depends not on the owner's after-tax income but on whether the worker will help the business make money.

4. Do Tax Cuts for Small Business Owners Create New Jobs?

The centerpiece of the Bush administration's economic policy has been large federal income tax cuts aimed mainly at top earners. These tax cuts account for much of the $2 trillion increase in the national debt projected to occur during the Bush presidency. They prompted a large group of Nobel laureates in economics to issue a statement last year condemning the administration's "reckless and extreme course that endangers the long-term economic health of our nation."

The question of whether to make the tax cuts permanent is still on the congressional agenda, making this an opportune moment to examine the president's argument in support of them.

President Bush never pretended that the tax cuts were needed to make life more comfortable for the well-to-do. After all, with the bulk of all pretax income gains having gone to top earners in recent years, this group has prospered as never before.

Rather, the president portrayed his tax cuts as the linchpin of his economic stimulus package. He argued that because most new jobs are created by small businesses, tax cuts to the owners of those businesses would stimulate robust employment growth. His policy thus rests implicitly on the premise that if business owners could afford to hire additional workers, they would. But whether owners can afford to hire is not the issue. What matters is whether hiring will increase their profits.

The basic hiring criterion, found in every introductory textbook (including those written by the president's own economic advisers), is straightforward: if the output of additional workers can be sold for at least enough to cover their salaries, they should be hired; otherwise not. If this criterion is met, hiring extra workers makes economic sense, no matter how poor a business owner may be. Conversely, if the criterion is not satisfied, hiring makes no economic sense, even for billionaire owners. The after-tax personal income of a business owner is irrelevant for hiring decisions.

The president's defenders might respond that business owners often need money up front to cover the hiring and training costs incurred before new workers can effectively contribute to extra production. The tax cuts put that money in their pockets. That is true but does nothing to alter the basic hiring rule.

Owners who used their tax cuts to finance the initial costs of new hiring would be acting, in effect, as their own bankers, lending money to themselves in the hope of future returns. The test for whether such internal loans make economic sense is exactly the same as the test for external loans.

A loan from a bank makes sense if the firm gains enough from hiring extra workers to cover not only their salaries but also repayment of the loan plus interest. Internal loans must meet the same standard. They are justified only if the firm gains enough from hiring extra workers to cover their salaries and repayment of the loan, including the interest that owners could have earned had they left their tax cuts in the bank. In hiring decisions, the implicit costs of internal loans have exactly the same economic standing as the explicit costs of external loans.

In brief, the president's claim that tax cuts to the owners of small businesses will stimulate them to hire more workers flies in the face of bedrock principles outlined in every introductory economics textbook.

A second way the Bush tax cuts might have stimulated employment is by inducing the wealthy to spend more on consumption. But a large share of the tax windfalls received by the wealthy are not spent in the short run. And even among those who are induced to spend more, the main effect is not increased demand for domestically produced goods and services, but rather increased bidding for choice oceanfront property and longer waiting lists for the new Porsche Carrera GT. Such spending does little to stimulate domestic employment.

Had the dollars required to finance the president's tax cuts been used in other ways, they would have made a real difference. Larger tax cuts for middle- and low-income families, for example, would have stimulated immediate new spending because the savings rates for most of these families are low. And their additional spending would have been largely for products made by domestic businesses, which would have led, in turn, to increased employment.

Grants to cash-starved state and local governments would have prevented layoffs of thousands of teachers and police officers. And many useful jobs could have been created directly. For instance, people could have been hired to scrutinize the cargo containers that currently enter the nation's ports uninspected.

Economists from both sides of the political aisle argued from the beginning that tax cuts for the wealthy made no sense as a policy for stimulating new jobs. And experience has proved them right. Total private employment was actually lower in January 2005 than in January 2001, the first time since the Great Depression that employment fell during a president's term of office.

New York Times, July 7, 2005

IN another brilliant rhetorical tactic, conservatives have used the term "death tax" to rally support for their efforts to repeal the estate tax, levied on heirs who receive extremely large bequests. One of the interesting puzzles in political science is that voters on even the lowest rungs of the income ladder voice strong support for this proposal, even though their heirs are less likely to owe estate taxes than to be struck by a meteorite. In the following selection, I argue that the estate tax is one of the least painful ways to pay for public services. I also cite evidence from an original survey suggesting that voter support for repeal of the estate tax is far shallower than it appears.

5. Is the Estate Tax Really As Bad As Rush Limbaugh Thinks?

The Bush administration has proposed permanent repeal of the estate tax, which people pay when they inherit money. Citing overwhelming support even among middle-class voters, some predict that the Senate will soon approve a repeal bill similar to the one the House passed last month.

But is support for repeal of the estate tax as broad as it appears? Survey respondents are typically told that repeal of the tax has been proposed and are then asked whether they favor such a move. Although two-thirds or more of respondents in most surveys respond affirmatively, this may tell us only that people find taxes of any sort unpleasant.

Well, sure, but that does not mean taxes are unnecessary. The alternative, after all, would be to have no army, which would eventually mean paying taxes to some other government whose army conquered us.

Repealing the estate tax would reduce federal revenues by close to $1 trillion from 2012 to 2021, according to the Center on Budget and Policy Priorities. This shortfall would require at least one of the following steps: raising income taxes, sales taxes, or other taxes; making further cuts in government services; or increasing the rate at which we borrow from China, Japan, and other countries. Additional borrowing would have to be repaid at market rates of interest, however, so the last option would also entail eventual tax increases or service cuts.

Many opponents of the estate tax argue that the revenue shortfall caused by its repeal will reduce bloated government. But in our current political system, spending cuts are more likely to take aim at basic public services than wasteful pork barrel projects. For example, President Bush, who campaigned as an enemy of government waste, recently proposed a 16 percent reduction in spending for veterans' health care, a 15 percent reduction for education and vocational training, and a 9.6 percent reduction for nutritional assistance for poor mothers with small children. So, unless we are willing to raise other taxes, repealing the estate tax will entail further cuts in valued services.

Would voters still favor repealing the estate tax if they took these repercussions into account? To find out, I asked the Survey Research Institute at Cornell University to administer two versions of a national telephone survey. In the first, respondents were asked simply whether they favored or opposed the Bush administration's proposal. Typical of the findings in similar surveys, these respondents favored repeal by almost three to one.

In the second version, respondents were reminded that the revenue shortfall from repealing the estate tax would entail raising other taxes, cutting government services, or increasing federal borrowing. Strikingly, these respondents opposed repeal by almost four to one. Although the sample sizes in both surveys were small (only 42 in the first group, 66 in the second), the odds of observing such a sweeping reversal by chance are remote.

If support for the abolition of the estate tax is an illusion, as it appears, is there an affirmative case for retaining this tax? Our basic goal is to pay for government services with a tax system that is as efficient, fair, and painless as possible. On all counts, it is difficult to imagine a better tax than the estate tax. Every dollar we collect from it is one less dollar we need to collect from some other tax that is worse in at least one of these dimensions.

GRAPHIC: A TALE OF TWO SURVEYS

(Random national telephone surveys performed by
Survey Research Institute, Cornell University)

Survey 1

The Bush administration has
proposed to eliminate the estate tax,
the tax people pay when they inherit
money.

    Do you favor or oppose this
proposal?

Survey Dates: April 29–May 6, 2005

Sample size: 42

Margin of error: 13.3%

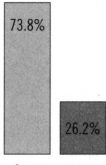

favor   oppose

Survey 2

The Bush administration has
proposed repeal of the estate tax,
the tax people pay when they
inherit money.

    The resulting revenue shortfall
would require at least one of the
following actions: raising other
taxes; implementing further cuts in
government services; or increasing the
rate at which the Federal government
has been borrowing money.

    All things considered, do
you favor or oppose the Bush
administration's proposal to
eliminate the estate tax?

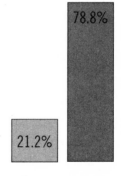

favor   oppose

Survey Dates: April 29–May 6, 2005

Sample size: 66

Margin of error: 9.9%

One important advantage of the estate tax is that it has virtually no negative effects on incentives. High income tax rates may discourage effort or investment. But who would become a slacker merely to avoid estate taxes? Because the estate tax allows income tax rates to be lower than they would otherwise be, it actually increases the incentive to invest and take risks.

Another attraction of the estate tax is that it works like a lawyer's contingency fee. Injured parties who could not otherwise afford access to the legal system can try to recover damages because lawyers are willing to work without pay if their client does not win. Similarly, the estate tax enables us to enjoy valuable public services that we would be happy to pay for if we knew we would end up wealthy, but that we might be reluctant to demand otherwise. With the estate tax, the surcharge kicks in only if we are lucky enough to be one of life's biggest winners.

The estate tax also provides an incentive for charitable giving, which reduces the need to pay for many public services with tax money. Recent estimates by the Brookings Institution and the Urban Institute suggest that its repeal may reduce such giving by as much as $15 billion a year. Finally, having estate taxes means paying lower taxes while we are alive, and taxes are generally more painful to the living than the dead.

Some opponents complain that the estate tax imposes an unreasonable burden on the owners of small businesses and farms. But inheritances of less than $1.5 million ($3 million for married couples) are currently untaxed, an exemption that will rise to $3.5 million ($7 million for couples) by 2009. Far fewer than 1 percent of heirs will ever pay a penny of estate tax; most of the revenue from estate taxes comes from inheritances larger than $10 million.

Many parents say they dislike the estate tax because they fear it will prevent them from doing all they can to ensure that their children are financially secure. Yet current exemption levels allow parents to leave their children more than enough to start a business, finance a premium education, buy a large house in a good school district, and still have several hundred thousand dollars left for a rainy day.

On reflection, would a parent really want them to inherit more than that? Old money has long been wary of the corrosive effect of guaranteed wealth on children's ability to set out on successful careers of their own, a concern that has prompted Warren E. Buffett and others to limit their bequests to their children. But even if Buffett were to change his mind, he could still leave an after-tax bequest of more than $20 billion under current tax laws.

In sum, although there are many taxes we ought to reduce or eliminate, the estate tax is not one of them. It is the closest thing to a perfect tax we have. And when the implications of its repeal are in plain view, most people seem to recognize their interest in keeping it. Even among Republicans, 70 percent opposed its repeal in the second version of my survey.

New York Times, May 12, 2005

TRICKLE-DOWN theory has had a powerful grip on political discourse since the Reagan administration. The theory holds that low taxes for the wealthy will stimulate economic growth whose fruits will eventually trickle down to everyone else. In the next selection, I explain why this claim has absolutely no basis in economic theory and is flatly contradicted by the historical record.

6. What Explains the Mysterious Appeal of Trickle-Down Theory?

When asked why he robbed banks, Willie Sutton famously replied, "Because that's where the money is." The same logic explains why John Edwards, the Democratic presidential candidate, called for higher taxes on top earners to underwrite his proposal for universal health coverage.

Providing universal coverage will be expensive. With the median wage, adjusted for inflation, lower now than in 1980, most middle-class families cannot afford additional taxes. In contrast, the top one-tenth of 1 percent of earners today make about four times as much as in 1980, while those higher up have enjoyed even larger gains. Chief executives of large American companies, for example, earn more than ten times what they did in 1980. In short, top earners are where the money is. Universal health coverage cannot happen unless they pay higher taxes.

Trickle-down theorists are quick to object that higher taxes would cause top earners to work less and take fewer risks, thereby stifling economic growth. In their familiar rhetorical flourish, they insist that a more progressive tax system would kill the geese that lay the golden eggs. On close examination, however, this claim is supported neither by economic theory nor by empirical evidence.

The surface plausibility of trickle-down theory comes from the time-honored belief that people respond to incentives. Because higher taxes on top earners reduce the reward for effort, it seems reasonable that they would induce people to work less, as trickle-down theorists claim. As every economics textbook makes clear, however, a decline in after-tax wages also exerts a second, opposing effect. By making people feel poorer, it provides them with an incentive to recoup their income loss by working harder than before. Economic theory says nothing about which of these offsetting effects may dominate.

If economic theory is unkind to trickle-down proponents, the lessons of experience are downright brutal. If lower real wages induce people to work shorter hours, then the opposite should be true when real wages increase. According to trickle-down theory, then, the cumulative effect of the last century's sharp rise in real wages should have been a significant increase in hours worked. In fact, however, the workweek is much shorter now than in 1900.

Trickle-down theory also predicts shorter workweeks in countries with lower real after-tax pay rates. Yet here too the numbers tell a different story. For example, even though chief executives in Japan earn less than one-fifth what their American counterparts do and face much higher marginal tax rates, Japanese executives do not log shorter hours.

Trickle-down theory also predicts a positive correlation between inequality and economic growth, the idea being that income disparities strengthen motivation to get ahead. Yet when researchers track the data within individual countries over time, they find a negative correlation. In the decades immediately after World War II, for example, income inequality was low by historical standards, yet growth rates in most industrial countries were extremely high. By contrast, in the years since 1973, growth rates have been only about half as large, even as inequality has been steadily rising.

The same pattern has been observed in cross-national data. For example, using data from the World Bank and the Organization for Economic Co-operation and Development for a sample of sixty-five industrial nations, the economists Alberto Alesina and Dani Rodrick found lower growth rates in countries where higher shares of national income went to the top 5 percent and the top 20 percent of earners. In contrast, larger shares for poor and middle-income groups were associated with higher growth rates. Again and again, the observed pattern is the opposite of the one predicted by trickle-down theory.

The trickle-down theorist's view of the world is nicely captured by a Donald Reilly cartoon depicting two well-fed executives nursing cocktails on a summer afternoon as they lounge on flotation devices in a pool. Pointing to himself, one says angrily to the other, "If those soak-the-rich birds get their way, I can tell you here's one coolie who'll stop putting his shoulder to the goddam wheel."

This portrait bears little resemblance to reality. In the 1950s, American executives earned far lower salaries and faced substantially higher marginal tax rates than they do today. Yet most of them competed energetically for higher rungs on the corporate ladder. The claim that slightly higher tax rates would cause today's executives to abandon that quest is simply not credible.

In the United States, trickle-down theory's insistence that a more progressive tax structure would compromise economic growth has long blocked attempts to provide valued public services. Thus, although every other industrial country provides universal health coverage, trickle-down theorists insist that the wealthiest country on earth cannot afford to do so. Elizabeth Edwards is battling her cancer with the full support of the world's most advanced medical system, yet millions of other Americans face similar battles without even minimal access to that system.

Low- and middle-income families are not the only ones who have been harmed by our inability to provide valued public services. For example, rich and poor alike would benefit from an expansion of the Energy Department's program to secure stockpiles of nuclear materials that remain poorly guarded in the former Soviet Union. Instead, the Bush administration has cut this program, even as terrorists actively seek to acquire nuclear weaponry.

The rich are where the money is. Many top earners would willingly pay higher taxes for public services that promise high value. Yet trickle-down theory, supported neither by theory nor evidence, continues to stand in the way. This theory is ripe for abandonment.

New York Times, April 12, 2007

THE final selection in this chapter is the column that elicited Rush Limbaugh's diatribe against me. It describes a one-line change in the tax code that would generate substantial new revenue without requiring voters to sacrifice anything they really care about.

7. Why Punish Savers?

In his memoir, Alan Greenspan joins a growing list of Republicans who now accuse President Bush of fiscal irresponsibility. As even veteran supply-siders now concede, the president's tax cuts have added hundreds of billions of dollars to the national debt.

Greenspan, who supported those cuts in testimony before the Senate Budget Committee in 2001, when he was the Federal Reserve chairman, now says he thought the president would be more disciplined about spending. It was an unreasonable expectation. Federal spending has risen during every modern presidency, even Ronald Reagan's.

Greenspan may have failed to convince critics that he bears no responsibility for the fiscal meltdown that is now under way, but his book has provoked long overdue debate about what caused the crisis and what might be done about it. As all serious participants in this debate now agree, no strategy can succeed without increasing federal revenue substantially. The leading Republican presidential aspirants, advocating further tax cuts, have elected to skip this debate. Their Democratic counterparts have proposed allowing the Bush tax cuts for top earners to expire as scheduled. That step alone, however, would not be nearly enough.

Given the political risk of proposing painful tax increases in an election year, many fear that the crisis will remain unresolved. Yet a simple remedy is at hand. By replacing federal income taxes with a steeply progressive consumption tax, the United States could erase the federal deficit, stimulate additional savings, pay for valuable public services, and reduce overseas borrowing—without requiring difficult sacrifices from taxpayers.

Under such a tax, people would report not only their income but also their annual savings, as many already do under 401(k) plans and other retirement accounts. A family's annual consumption is simply the difference between its income and its annual savings. That amount, minus a standard deduction—say, $30,000 for a family of four—would be the family's taxable consumption. Rates would start low, like 10 percent. A family that earned $50,000 and saved $5,000 would thus have taxable consumption of $15,000. It would pay only

$1,500 in tax. Under the current system of federal income taxes, this family would pay about $3,000 a year.

As taxable consumption rises, the tax rate on additional consumption would also rise. With a progressive income tax, marginal tax rates cannot rise beyond a certain threshold without threatening incentives to save and invest. Under a progressive consumption tax, however, higher marginal tax rates actually strengthen those incentives.

Consider a family that spends $10 million a year and is deciding whether to add a $2 million wing to its mansion. If the top marginal tax rate on consumption were 100 percent, the project would cost $4 million. The additional tax payment would reduce the federal deficit by $2 million. Alternatively, the family could scale back, building only a $1 million addition. Then it would pay $1 million in additional tax and could deposit $2 million in savings. The federal deficit would fall by $1 million, and the additional savings would stimulate investment, promoting growth. Either way, the nation would come out ahead with no real sacrifice required of the wealthy family, because when all build larger houses, the result is merely to redefine what constitutes acceptable housing. With a consumption tax in place, most neighbors would also scale back the new wings on their mansions.

A progressive consumption tax would also reduce the growing financial pressures confronting middle-class families. Top earners, having received not only the greatest income gains over the last three decades but also substantial tax cuts, have been building larger houses simply because they have more money. Those houses have shifted the frame of reference for people with slightly lower incomes, leading them to build larger as well. The resulting expenditure cascade has affected families at all income levels.

The median new house in the United States, for example, now has over 2,300 square feet, over 40 percent more than in 1979, even though real median family earnings have risen little since then. The problem is not that middle-income families are trying to "keep up with the Gateses." Rather, these families feel pressure to spend beyond what they can comfortably afford because more expensive neighborhoods tend to have better schools. A family that spends less than its peers on housing must thus send its children to lower-quality schools.

Some people worry that tax incentives for reduced consumption might throw the economy into recession. But total spending, not just consumption, determines output and employment. If a progressive consumption tax were phased in gradually, its main effect would be to shift spending from consumption to investment, causing productivity and incomes to rise faster.

Should a recession occur, a temporary cut in consumption taxes would provide a much more powerful stimulus than the traditional temporary cut in income taxes can. People would benefit from a temporary consumption tax cut only if they spent more right away. In contrast, consumers who fear that they might lose their jobs in a recession are often reluctant to spend the dollars they are no longer paying as income tax.

Failure to address the current fiscal crisis is not an attractive option. With baby boomers retiring and most voters now favoring universal health coverage, budget shortfalls will grow sharply. Annual borrowing from abroad, now more than $800 billion, will also increase, causing further declines in the slumping dollar. And the personal savings rate, which has been negative for the last two years, will fall still further, causing future reductions in economic growth.

The progressive consumption tax is perhaps the only instrument that can reverse these trends at acceptable political cost. It has been endorsed by a long list of distinguished economists of varying political orientations. It was proposed in the Senate in 1995 by Sam Nunn, the Georgia Democrat then serving his final term, and Pete V. Domenici, Republican of New Mexico, who called it the unlimited savings allowance tax. In short, this tax is not a radical idea.

Although the Bush tax cuts for the nation's wealthiest families threaten American economic prosperity, they have done little for their ostensible beneficiaries. When the wealthy spend millions of dollars on ever more elaborate coming-of-age parties for their children, they only raise the bar that defines a special occasion. Even purely in terms of self-interest, they and their families would have fared much better if the money had been spent to repair aging bridges and inspect the cargo containers that enter the nation's ports.

New York Times, October 7, 2007

2

Do Nice Guys Always Finish Last?

The sociologist Harvey Hornstein once performed an experiment in which he dropped wallets on the sidewalks of New York City. Each contained a small amount of cash, various cards and laundry receipts, and the name and address of the wallet's ostensible owner. Traditional economic models, which portray people as self-interested in a narrow sense, predict that people who find these wallets will keep the cash. Yet more than half of the wallets were returned through the mail, usually anonymously, with the cash intact.

Traditional economic models also predict that people will not vote in presidential elections because voting entails costs and no individual's vote has ever tipped the outcome in any state, not even the bitterly contested battle over Florida in 2000. The same models predict that people will not leave tips in restaurants they don't expect to visit again. But although these predictions sometimes hold, counterexamples abound.

Most economists realize that self-interest is not the only important motive. To explain why people vote, we could simply assume they derive satisfaction from doing so. But many economists cite the "crankcase oil" objection. Suppose we saw a man drain the crankcase oil from his car, drink it, and then writhe in agony before dying minutes later. We could "explain" his behavior after the fact by assuming a powerful preference for drinking crankcase oil. A theory that can explain virtually any bizarre behavior does not yield testable predictions and is therefore not really a viable scientific theory.

But moral sentiments like sympathy and a sense duty have little in common with a taste for crankcase oil, since it is widely known that the former sentiments influence people's choices in at least some situations. The selections in this chapter explore how different the world looks once we abandon the economist's self-interest straitjacket.

THE first selection considers the question of whether what we teach shapes what we do. Teaching about self-interest, not surprisingly, seems to make people more likely to behave in self-interested ways.

8. Does What We Teach Shape What We Do?

A *New Yorker* cartoon depicts an elderly, well-heeled gentleman taking his grandson for a walk in the woods. "It's good to know about trees," he tells the boy. "Just remember, nobody ever made big money knowing about trees."

If the man's advice was not inspired directly by the economist's rational-actor model, it could have been. This model assumes that people are selfish in the narrow sense. It may be nice to know about trees, but the world out there is bitterly competitive, and that those who do not ruthlessly pursue their own interests are likely to be swept aside by others who do.

To be sure, self-interest is an important human motive, and the self-interest model has well-established explanatory power. When energy prices rise, for example, people are more likely to buy hybrid vehicles and add extra insulation in their attics.

But some economists assert that self-interest explains virtually all behavior. As Gordon Tullock of George Mason University has written, for example, "the average human being is about 95 percent selfish in the narrow sense of the term." Is he right? Or do we often heed social and cultural norms that urge us to set aside self-interest in the name of some greater good?

When searching for examples that contradict the predictions of standard economic models, a good rule of thumb is to start in France. During my recent sabbatical in Paris, I encountered many such examples, but one in particular stands out. On a mid-November afternoon, I asked my neighborhood wine merchant to recommend a good champagne. It was the week before Thanksgiving, and my wife and I had invited a few American friends to our apartment for a turkey dinner.

He just happened to have an excellent one on sale for only eighteen euros (normally 24 euros). Fine, I said, and then asked if he could also recommend a bottle of cassis, since some of our guests would want a kir royale—a cocktail of cassis and champagne. In that case, he said, I would have no need for the high-quality champagne, because no one would be able to tell the difference once it was mixed with cassis. Well, then, what should I buy? He brought back a bottle that he said would be just right for the purpose.

That particular champagne, however, was not on sale. When he told me it was twenty euros per bottle—two euros more than the better one—an awkward pause ensued. Though I thought I knew the answer, I felt I had to ask whether a kir royale would taste worse if made with the better champagne. He assured me it would not. And because I knew that some of us would be drinking our champagne straight, I bought several bottles of the better one. He did not protest, but I could feel him reclassify me as yet another American barbarian.

For many French, the logic of the self-interest model is trumped by an aesthetic principle about what champagnes are right for specific applications. This particular principle leads to a better outcome over all, because it directs the best champagne to the uses in which quality matters most. Even though I personally was better off for ignoring the merchant's advice (because I got to drink a better champagne and spent less), at least some of the better champagne I bought was wasted.

France is, of course, not the only place in which the self-interest model's predictions fall short. Most Americans, for example, leave tips even after dining in restaurants they will never visit again. We take the trouble to vote in presidential elections, even though no single individual's vote has ever changed the outcome in any state. We make anonymous donations to charity. From society's perspective, our willingness to forgo self-interest in such instances leads to better outcomes than when we all act in a purely selfish manner.

Does what we believe about human motivation matter? In an experimental study of private contributions to a common project, two sociologists from the University of Wisconsin, Gerald Marwell and Ruth Ames, found that first-year graduate students in economics contributed an average of less than half the amount contributed by students from other disciplines.

Other studies have found that repeated exposure to the self-interest model makes selfish behavior more likely. In one experiment, for example, the cooperation rates of economics majors fell short of those of nonmajors, and the difference grew the longer the students had been in their respective majors.

My point is not that my fellow economists are wrong to stress the importance of self-interest. But those who insist that it is the only important human motive are missing something important. Even more troubling, the narrow self-interest model, which encourages us to expect the worst in others, often brings out the worst in us as well.

Perhaps the theories of human behavior embraced by other disciplines influence their practitioners in similar ways. A core principle of behavioral biology, for example, is that males are far more likely than females to engage in "extrapair copulations." Does teaching this model year after year make male biologists more likely to stray?

Several years ago, I attended a dinner with a group of biologists that included a married couple. After describing the research about how economics training appears to inhibit cooperation, I asked whether anyone had ever done a study of whether males in biology were more likely than scholars from other disciplines to be unfaithful to their partners. The uncomfortable silence that greeted my question made me wonder whether I had stumbled onto a data point relevant for such a study.

But if biologists are like economists in being influenced by their own theories, they are different from us in another respect: their most cherished hypothesis is less likely than ours to be contradicted by the French.

New York Times, February 17, 2005

CAN nobler motives survive in bitterly competitive environments? Although the world would be a nicer place if everyone showed respect for the legitimate interests of others, many Darwinians argue that the forces of natural selection will eventually drive such people to extinction. In the next selection, I suggest a simple answer to the question of why that appears not to have happened.

9. How Do Ethical People Survive?

With steroid violations and accounting chicanery so much in the news, one begins to wonder how honest individuals still manage to survive in competitive domains.

Sanctions against violators obviously help, but what about the countless situations in which cheaters face little possibility of being caught and punished? Is it quixotic to hope that honesty will prevail in these situations?

Economic analysis suggests that this question has a different answer in the world of sports than in the world of business.

At first glance, the factors that motivate cheating seem to reinforce pessimism about its inevitability. Although some athletes take steroids to gain an unfair advantage over their rivals, evidence suggests that most drug users believe that everyone else is cheating. To these athletes, to refrain from cheating may actually seem unfair.

Corporate misconduct stems from a similar mix of motives. Without doubt, some cheaters are driven primarily by greed and raw ambition. But many others are just trying to avoid falling behind their rivals.

Given the Darwinian logic of competition, honest competitors—those who don't cheat even when no one is looking—should be destined for extinction, both in sports and in business. But there is an important and often overlooked difference between these two domains.

In sports, dishonest competitors lose ground only in the relatively rare instances in which they are caught and punished. But in business, even cheaters who are never caught often pay a price. It is not an explicit price, but rather a failure to be eligible for certain valuable opportunities.

In particular, business managers with a reputation for cheating are less likely to be promoted into positions that require trust. A business owner considering whether to open a branch in a distant city where close supervision is impossible, for example, may know that the venture is likely to be highly profitable only with an honest manager running it.

In this case, dishonest candidates suffer not because they were caught and punished for cheating, but rather because they were not offered responsible jobs at premium salaries in the first place. The critical requirement for honesty to survive is that business owners must be able to identify those who will perform honestly even when cheating cannot be detected. Can they do that?

Imagine yourself returning from a crowded concert to discover that you have lost an envelope containing $5,000 in cash. (You had cashed a check for that amount to pay for a used car you planned to buy the next morning.) Your name and address were written on the envelope. Can you think of anyone, not related to you by blood or marriage, who you feel certain would return your cash if he or she found it?

Most people say they can, and considerable evidence supports them. In one experiment involving a game of trust, for example, strangers of only brief acquaintance were asked to predict which of their partners would cheat them. The players they identified were more than twice as likely as others to be cheaters.

Character judgments regarding longer-term acquaintances should be even more accurate. If the people who make promotion decisions in business can make sufficiently accurate character judgments, honest candidates have an inside track for promotion into well-paying positions that require trust. That explains why honesty is often a winning strategy in business.

The situation is fundamentally different with athletes. Suppose there is an undetectable drug that enhances performance in the hundred-meter dash. Now imagine a sprinter known by all to be scrupulously honest, someone who would not take the drug, even if there were no chance of getting caught. This sprinter is no more likely, by virtue of his honesty, to win a race.

On the contrary, because at least some sprinters can be expected to cheat, he stands a better chance of losing. After retiring from sports, he may have a leg up as an applicant for a job that requires trust. But that won't help him win any races.

Beliefs matter. If people believe cheating is inevitable, there will be more of it; if honesty in business is a winning strategy, it is good for people to realize that. Of course, the mere fact that honest people may prosper in competitive business environments provides no guarantee that they will do so. In every domain, we will continue to need strict rules and sanctions to help keep misconduct at bay.

Even so, things aren't as bad as many seem to think. Regarding the criteria for success, George Burns once said, "Acting is all about honesty; if you can fake that, you've got it made." Employers are no doubt fooled some of the time, but faking honesty is easier said than done. By the time people are considered for positions that require trust, their employers are likely to have considerable insight into their character.

In business, there is indeed great advantage in being seen as honest. The best way to gain that advantage, it seems, is to be honest.

New York Times, August 4, 2005

CLEARLY many people do the right thing even when they could break the rules with no possibility of apprehension and punishment. Imagine a world in which everyone was essentially honest. Go ahead. Try. In such a world, would it be prudent to leave your doors unlocked? In the next selection, written during George W. Bush's first term, I explore why honest behavior would be unlikely to survive if everyone knew that violators of ethical norms would never be punished.

10. If People Were Basically Honest, Would Sanctions Be Necessary?

From his approach to pollution abatement as Texas governor to his approach to corporate malfeasance as president, George W. Bush promoted voluntary compliance. Explaining his initial opposition to the strict criminal sanctions in the corporate fraud statute passed in 2002, for example, he conceded that although tougher laws might help, "ultimately, the ethics of American business depend on the conscience of America's business leaders."

There are indeed limits to the law's ability to regulate human behavior, and public officials do well to try to nurture our inclination to do the right thing. But an emphasis on voluntary compliance overlooks the critical role of enforcement measures in society's efforts to curb narrow self-interest for the common good. Without such measures, we must ask those who comply voluntarily to shoulder an unfair burden.

The difficulty is illustrated by the forces confronting honest executives as they weigh how to report company earnings. They know that many entries in the company's financial statements necessarily entail subjective judgments. Some, for instance, hinge on estimates and assumptions about the future, others on imperfect models for imputing monetary values to nonmarket assets. Consequently a broad range of earnings estimates could be defended as reasonable.

Therein lies the problem, because a company's ability to finance its future growth depends strongly on how its current reported earnings compare with those of rival firms. It is on this basis that capital markets infer which firms are most likely to succeed. Stock prices often fall sharply in the short run for those reporting relatively low current earnings, increasing their risk of failure in the long run. Under the circumstances, it is difficult to see how even the most scrupulous executives could justify calculating their company's earnings on the basis of strictly neutral, let alone pessimistic, assumptions. On the plausible forecast that most other companies will report earnings near the optimistic end of the reasonable range, failure to do likewise would understate the company's true prospects.

Worse still, this situation is unstable, because the standards that define acceptable accounting judgments are inherently dependent on context. When almost all companies issue optimistic earnings reports, such reports come to be viewed as normal. Even the most cautious executives then feel pressure to report their earnings more aggressively, creating room for their more aggressive counterparts to push the envelope still further.

Given this dynamic and the enormous sums at stake in the battle for corporate survival, careful monitoring and stiff sanctions against violators are essential. It is one thing to ask people to forgo ill-gotten gain but quite another to ask them to commit economic suicide. Many of WorldCom's competitors were injured, some even driven into bankruptcy, by their failure to match WorldCom's aggressive accounting practices. (WorldCom itself would still be flying high except for the sudden collapse of revenue in the telecommunications industry.)

A similar logic applies to all other forms of malfeasance in the marketplace. If athletes can gain ground at the expense of their rivals by taking steroids without penalty, many will do so. And if people can claim questionable tax exemptions without penalty, many will do so. These actions pressure others to respond in kind, which in turn shifts the standards that define acceptable conduct.

If we want people to restrain themselves for the common good, the sacrifices we demand must be equitable. To ask athletes not to use steroids in the absence of effective sanctions, however, is to penalize those who comply while rewarding those who don't. To ask people to be scrupulous in their tax filings in an audit-free environment is to reduce the effective tax rate for dishonest taxpayers while increasing it for honest ones.

Congress was wise to include criminal sanctions in its recent corporate fraud legislation. Major League Baseball would be wise to include frequent random testing and stiff penalties against violators in the steroid ban it is currently considering. And President Bush might want to rethink the wisdom of the IRS staff and budget cuts that have reduced the tax audit rate by more than half since 1996.

As Adam Smith was well aware, the invisible hand of the marketplace does not always produce the greatest good for all. When individual and social interests conflict, calls for voluntary compliance must be supplemented by sanctions that are potent enough to matter. As President Reagan aptly put it, "Trust, but verify."

New York Times, August 24, 2002

IN the following selection, written during the 2008 presidential primaries, I tackle the question of why people volunteer their time and money for political campaigns. The standard economic explanation—that donors are rewarded with jobs and contracts—may explain some cases but doesn't fit the millions of donors whose small gifts hold no promise of a quid pro quo.

11. Why Was JFK's "Ask Not" Appeal So Effective?

Traditional economic models assume that people are self-interested in the narrow sense. If "homo economicus" (the stereotypical rational actor in these models) finds a wallet on the sidewalk, he keeps the cash inside. He doesn't leave tips after dining in restaurants that he will never visit again. And he would never vote in a presidential election, much less donate money or time to a presidential campaign.

This posture stems from the so-called free rider problem, a cornerstone of rational choice theory. The problem, as described by Mancur Olson in his classic book, *The Logic of Collective Action*, is that even those who share a presidential candidate's policy goals will reap no significant material advantage by donating their time or money. After all, with cash donations legally capped at $2,300, even donors who give the maximum have no realistic hope of influencing an election's outcome. Nor can any individual volunteer—even one whose efforts resulted in hundreds of additional votes for his candidate—realistically hope to tip an election.

Although the logic of the free rider problem may seem compelling, people's behavior strikingly contradicts many of its predictions. In January 2008, for example, the Obama presidential campaign raised over $32 million from more than 250,000 individual donors and sent an even larger number of volunteers into the field. Other campaigns have benefited in similar, if less spectacular ways from their supporters' willingness to set aside narrow self-interest.

Die-hard proponents of self-interest models sometimes counter that campaign volunteers reap a variety of personal advantages. They often meet interesting people, for example, or they may learn about attractive employment opportunities. Major donors are often rewarded with ambassadorships or other prominent positions when their candidate wins.

Fair points, especially when applied to bundlers—donors who assemble contributions totaling hundreds of thousands of dollars from friends and associates. But what about the millions of others who make small cash donations? The elderly South Carolina woman who sent her chosen candidate a money order for $3.01 surely did not expect to be appointed ambassador to the Court of St. James. And what about the volunteers who staff phone banks from home or perform other tasks that offer little opportunity for social interaction?

When viewed through the lens of traditional self-interest models, such behavior is equivalent to the impossible geological phenomenon of a river flowing uphill. It often seems to entail a yearning to participate in something larger than oneself and is by no means limited to the political domain. Fans of sports teams, for example, often seem oblivious to the standard cost-benefit calculations, as do the followers of certain rock bands.

Researchers at the intersection of economics, psychology, sociology, and other disciplines have said interesting things about the anomaly inherent in collective action. Albert O. Hirschman, an economist at the Institute for Advanced Study at Princeton, was one of the first to grapple with it. In his 1982 book *Shifting Involvements* he acknowledges that self-interest indeed appears to be the dominant human motive in some eras. But over time, he argues, many people begin to experience disappointment as they continue to accumulate material goods. When consumption standards escalate, people must work harder just to hold their place. Stress levels rise. People become less willing to devote resources to the public sphere, which begins to deteriorate. Against this backdrop, disenchanted consumers become increasingly receptive to appeals from the organizers of social movements.

Eventually, Hirschman argues, a tipping point is reached. In growing numbers, people peel away from their private rat race to devote energy to collective goals. The free rider problem ceases to inhibit them, not only because they now assign less value to private consumption but also because they find satisfaction in the very act of contributing to the common good. Activities viewed as costs by self-interest models are thus seen as benefits instead.

In Hirschman's account, a similar dynamic governs the pursuit of collective action. Although social movements often command substantial allegiance for many years, at some point their supporters' commitment begins to falter. One reason for this, perhaps, is that the bar that defines morally praiseworthy behavior shifts with context. When growing numbers of people actively dedicate themselves to the pursuit of civic virtue, it becomes harder to earn moral approval by volunteering. When some discouraged volunteers abandon the social movement to resume pursuing private accumulation, remaining adherents feel increasing pressure to do likewise. And at that point the cycle is set to repeat.

From an informal survey of twentieth-century American social movements, Hirschman concluded that these cycles have an average duration of about twenty years. But sometimes patterns take much longer to recur.

Many people have likened the response to Barack Obama's appeal for civic engagement to the response to similar appeals by President John F. Kennedy during the 1960s. Then as now, many economists were skeptical. The Nobel laureate Milton Friedman, for example, began the opening chapter of his 1962 book, *Capitalism and Freedom,* by quoting a famous passage from Kennedy's inaugural address: "Ask not what your country can do for you, ask what you can do for your country." Friedman dismissed the statement as not "worthy of the ideals of free men in a free society."

"The free man," he wrote, "will ask neither what his country can do for him, nor what he can do for his country."

Some economists seem similarly baffled by the exuberance inspired by the Obama candidacy. But while homo economicus may not respond to calls for sacrifice for the common good, many people plainly do.

Self-interest is an important human motive, perhaps even the most important motive much of the time. But it is never the only important motive. And during some moments in history, narrow self-interest models miss the essential story line completely. This may be one of those moments.

New York Times, February 10, 2008

WHEN pharmaceutical companies donate millions of dollars to re-elect congressmen and senators who then vote for legislation that prohibits the government from negotiating prescription drug discounts for Medicare recipients, the potential conflict of interest is apparent. Champions of good government have long advocated public financing of political campaigns as a way of eliminating this conflict. In the final selection in this chapter, I explain why constitutional constraints appear to have made this approach unworkable.

12. Can Laws Curb the Corrupting Influence of Money in Politics?

When Barack Obama rejected public financing for his presidential campaign, he caught heavy flak from all sides. Critics, including some of his most ardent supporters, complained that he was willing to abandon the cause of good government to gain a financial edge.

What the critics have ignored is that truly effective campaign finance reform has been precluded by First Amendment concerns. Given that constraint, the Obama campaign's approach may offer the only realistic possibility of limiting the corrupting influence of money in politics.

Many champions of good government say they favor public financing because campaign spending is wasteful. It's a fair point. After all, campaign spending is driven by the same logic that governs a military arms race. But while the competition to amass bigger and more powerful weapons generates waste on a truly grand scale, the waste from campaign spending is a small fraction of 1 percent of national income. The spending itself is not the problem. The far more compelling rationale for campaign finance reform is to prevent the conflicts of interest that produce bad laws and policies.

Even in the face of current campaign finance legislation, politicians remain subject to such conflicts. Scores of members of Congress, for example, accepted contributions from the same pharmaceutical companies that reaped millions of dollars of additional profit from the provision in Medicare Part D legislation that prevented the government from negotiating discount prescription prices for beneficiaries.

Most of these legislators would deny any conflict, saying the provision they supported had somehow served the public interest. That's not surprising—few of us like to acknowledge possible vulnerability to conflicts of interest. But we are quick to recognize that others are subject to them, which explains the perennial attraction of legislation to limit the role of money in politics.

In legislative matters, however, the devil is in the details. Both the Federal Election Campaign Act (amended in the aftermath of Watergate in 1974) and the more recent Bipartisan Campaign Reform Act of 2002 (popularly known as McCain-Feingold) have faced numerous First Amendment challenges, and more are pending. Although the Supreme Court has affirmed the legality of placing contribution and expenditure limits on candidates who accept public financing, it has ruled against imposing similar limits on independent advocacy groups.

Because political expression occupies such a hallowed place in the American constitutional tradition, the court's First Amendment concerns won't vanish. Voicing one's opinions effectively in a political campaign requires money. So the law can't eliminate the influence of money in politics without also preventing people from making their political views heard.

At the same time, it is vitally important to prevent donors from buying laws and policies in violation of the public trust.

The harsh reality is that free speech and good government are conflicting goals. When forced to choose, the Supreme Court has essentially sided with free speech. Recent decisions by the Roberts court suggest an even stronger tilt in that direction.

That is the crucial backdrop to the 2008 campaign. Despite the McCain-Feingold law, the First Amendment constraint had essentially made it impossible to impose effective legal limits on campaign spending. As the year unfolded, however, the Obama campaign demonstrated the possibility not only of remaining financially competitive but also of raising record sums by relying primarily on small donations from individuals. (Disclosure: I'm one of those contributors.)

This was a significant change as voters took matters into their own hands. For them to be able to avoid candidates who are beholden to large contributors, the law need only require full public disclosure of campaign contributions, a step that poses no threat to the First Amendment.

Senator Obama's fund-raising totals caught many observers off guard. After all, traditional economic models suggest that a campaign financed by small individual donations shouldn't go far. The problem, according to these models, is that because a campaign's fate is essentially independent of any given small donation, no individual donor can expect to have any influence. Yet many small donors seem undeterred by that logic.

Campaign finance reform laws notwithstanding, political campaign contributions from large donors have grown explosively in recent decades. Because the marketplace has become more competitive, corporations are under greater pressure to bend the rules to their own advantage. In this effort, the corporate side has had victories like Medicare Part D, the so-called Enron loophole, and the deregulation of the financial industry. But the public has often paid a heavy price.

To be sure, the Obama campaign's achievement does nothing to reduce the scale of campaign budgets. And the fact that small donors can finance successful campaigns does not guarantee that champions of good government will prevail. A charismatic tyrant, for example, might be a successful fund-raiser. Current campaign finance laws, which allow but do not require public financing, provide no protection against the emergence of such a tyrant.

The Obama campaign has demonstrated that if enough people are willing to withhold donations to politicians who rely on large private contributions, voters have the power to eliminate the fundamental conflicts of interest that have corrupted American politics in recent decades. Because of the First Amendment constraint, that's something McCain-Feingold and other campaign finance laws simply cannot deliver by themselves.

New York Times, July 6, 2008

3

Money and Happiness

Although the roots of utilitarianism have been traced back as far as the Greek philosopher Epicurus, its modern form emerged in the writings of the eighteenth-century English philosopher Jeremy Bentham. He argued that the right course of action is the one that results in the greatest balance of pleasure over pain for everyone. Since Bentham's day, economists have used the term "utility" to describe what individuals and societies seek to maximize. Unlike happiness, which is commonly associated with positive emotions, utility is a broader concept used to rank different outcomes. Thus, if a person or society prefers one situation to another, the first situation is said to yield higher utility than the second. But even though utility and happiness do not always move together, they are strongly correlated. This is no surprise, since most people prefer to be happy rather than unhappy.

Many economists take it as given that choice reveals preference. For example, choosing flank steak over roast chicken when the two dishes cost the same is generally taken as evidence that the beef dish yields higher utility, at least on that occasion. This framework may help explain why economists are more likely than other social scientists to exhibit an affinity for libertarianism. Libertarians believe that individuals are in the best position to know which alternative works best for them. The best way to maximize total utility, many economists believe, is to put as much money into people's hands as possible and then let them spend it as they see fit. And since utility and happiness generally move together, the same arrangements that maximize utility should also tend to maximize happiness.

All this seemed so obvious to economists that until recently few of my colleagues showed any interest in studies of the link between happiness and income. But that link has become a subject of growing interest in recent years. For one thing, evidence has been accumulating that people don't always make intelligent decisions about how to spend their income. So it now seems more of an open question whether having more income makes people happier.

A second factor driving interest in the income-happiness relationship is economists' increasing awareness that the combined effects of decisions that make sense from each individual's point of view often do not add up to a sensible outcome for the groups to which they belong. At a cocktail party, for example, it is rational for an individual to speak louder if his conversation partner is having trouble hearing. Yet when all speak louder, the effect is to raise the ambient noise level, making it more difficult to hear than before.

THE selections in this chapter address various aspects of the link between money and happiness. The first focuses on an article written by John Maynard Keynes, widely considered the most brilliant economist of the twentieth century. Keynes thought income matters for happiness, but only to the extent that pressing material needs remain unmet. Projecting the twentieth century's rapid productivity growth into the future, he worried that the grandchildren of people in his generation would struggle to find ways to fill their days, since it would be possible for them to meet their needs by working only a few hours each week. Although productivity indeed grew as predicted, Keynes needn't have fretted.

13. Is Human Desire Boundless?

Productivity growth has raised living standards in the United States more than forty-fold since 1790. In his 1930 essay "Economic Possibilities for Our Grandchildren," John Maynard Keynes speculated about how continued productivity growth might transform our lives. Like many other distinguished thinkers, both before him and after, he predicted that people would have great difficulty filling their days once it became unnecessary to spend more than a token amount of time working.

This concern seems comical in retrospect. Productivity's upward trajectory has become even steeper in the decades since 1930, yet people are working just as hard as ever.

How could Keynes, the most influential economist of the twentieth century, have made such an absurd prediction? It would be one thing if he had merely overlooked the possibility of boundless human desire. Yet he explicitly considered this possibility, only to dismiss it.

Keynes wrote that human needs fall into two classes: basic (or absolute) needs, which are independent of what others have, and relative needs, which we feel "only if their satisfaction lifts us above, makes us feel superior to, our fellows."

Keynes granted that although needs rooted in a desire for superiority may indeed be insatiable, this is not true of absolute needs. And seeing absolute needs as more important by far, he concluded, "A point may soon be reached, much sooner perhaps than we are all aware of, when these needs are satisfied in the sense that we prefer to devote our further energies to noneconomic purposes."

Keynes was surely correct that only a small fraction of total spending is prompted by the desire to flaunt personal superiority. He was profoundly mistaken, however, in seeing this desire as the only source of insatiable demands.

Decisions to spend are also driven by perceptions of quality, the desire for which knows no bounds. But quality is a relative concept. The same car that would have been deemed as having brisk acceleration and sure handling by drivers in Keynes's day, for example, would be much less charitably evaluated by today's drivers, even those with no desire to outdo their neighbors.

An economist's formal mathematical model of the demand for automobile quality would incorporate an explicit comparison of a car's features with the corresponding features of other cars in the same local environment. Cars whose features scored positively in such comparisons would be seen as having high quality, for which consumers would be willing to pay a premium. In purely mathematical terms, such a model would be essentially identical to one based on a desire not to own quality for its own sake, but rather to outdo others.

Yet the subjective impressions conveyed by these two descriptions could hardly be more different. To demand quality for its own sake is to be a discerning buyer. But to flaunt one's superiority is to be a boor, a social moron. Such people exist, but most of us manage to avoid them most of the time, which suggests that they are rare.

Perceptions of quality influence the demand for virtually every good, including even basic goods like food. When a couple goes out for an anniversary dinner, for example, the thought of feeling superior to others probably never enters their minds. Their goal is to share a memorable meal, a quintessentially relative concept—a meal that stands out from other meals.

The standards that define a memorable meal are elastic. When my wife and I were living in Paris a few years ago, we went out to dinner with well-to-do friends who were visiting from the United States. The restaurant we chose had a good reputation and, by our standards, was not cheap. My wife and I enjoyed our meal enormously, but our friends found theirs disappointing. I'm confident they were not trying to impress us or make us feel inferior. By virtue of their substantially higher income, they had simply grown accustomed to a higher standard of cuisine.

There are no obvious limits to the escalation of quality standards. For example, dinner for two at Sketch in London can easily top $500, even if you choose the least expensive offering on the wine list. No one had to spend that much to enjoy a memorable meal in Keynes's day. But if productivity keeps growing, it is just a matter of time before the price of a special meal becomes twice that amount. As we approach the frontiers of existing quality standards, even minor improvements can be enormously expensive.

Until recently, for example, the Porsche 911 Turbo was considered perhaps the best all-around sports car on the market. Priced at over $120,000, it handles impeccably and has blistering acceleration.

But in 2004, Porsche raised the bar by introducing its Carrera GT, which handles slightly better than the Turbo and beats its 0-to-60 time by two-tenths of a second. People who really care about cars find these small improvements exciting. To get them, however, they must pay almost four times the price of the Turbo.

By placing the desire to outdo others at the heart of his description of insatiable demands, Keynes relegated such demands to the periphery. But the desire for higher quality has no natural limits. Keynes and others were wrong to imagine a two-hour workweek enabling us to buy everything we want. That hasn't happened and never will.

New York Times, September 28, 2006

A WIDELY reported finding from the happiness literature is that measured happiness levels change very little as incomes grow over time. Although recent studies have challenged this finding, many interpret it to mean that economic growth is no longer an important objective for countries that have already achieved high per capita incomes. But for reasons I describe in the next selection, this conclusion simply does not follow.

14. Is Happiness the Only Important Welfare Measure?

Does money buy happiness? The rapidly expanding literature on what determines subjective well-being suggests a negative answer to this timeless question. Studies consistently find, for example, that when the income of everyone in a community grows over time, conventional measures of well-being show little change.

Many critics of economic growth interpret this finding to imply that continued economic growth should no longer be a policy goal in developed countries. They argue that if money buys happiness, it is relative, not absolute income that matters. As incomes grow, people quickly adapt to their new circumstances, showing no enduring gains in measured happiness. Growth makes the poor happier in low-income countries, critics concede, but not in developed countries, where those at the bottom continue to experience relative deprivation.

All true. But these statements do not imply that economic growth no longer matters in wealthy countries. The reason, in a nutshell, is that happiness and welfare, though related, are not the same. Growth enables us to expand medical research and other activities that enhance human welfare but have little effect on measured happiness levels.

Subjective well-being is typically measured from responses to survey questions like, "All things considered, how satisfied are you with your life these days?" People's responses are informative. They tend to be consistent over time and are highly correlated with assessments of them made by their friends. Positive self-assessments are strongly linked with behaviors indicating psychological health. Thus people who report high levels of subjective well-being are more likely to initiate social contacts with friends and more likely to respond to requests for assistance from strangers. They are less likely than others to suffer from psychosomatic illnesses, seek psychological counseling, or attempt suicide.

In short, self-assessments of subjective well-being tell us something important about human welfare. Yet the mere fact that they do not ratchet up over time provides little reason to question the desirability of economic growth.

The purpose of the human motivational system, according to psychologists, is not to make people feel happy but rather to motivate actions that promote successful life outcomes. To be effective, this system should be flexible and adaptive, which it is. For example, people who become disabled typically experience deep depression after their accident but often adapt surprisingly quickly, soon reporting a mix of moods similar to what they had experienced before. Lottery winners invariably experience joy on receiving their windfall but often describe such feelings as fleeting.

Since life is a continuing competitive struggle, this is as it should be. Accident victims who recover their psychological footing quickly will function more effectively in their new circumstances than those who dwell on their misfortune. Windfall recipients who quickly recover their hunger for more will compete more effectively than those who linger in complacent euphoria.

A Holocaust survivor once told me that his existence in the camps took place in two separate psychological spaces. In one, he was acutely aware of the unspeakable horror of his situation. But in the other, life seemed eerily normal. In this second space, each day presented challenges, and days in which he coped successfully felt much like the good days of the past. To survive, he explained, it was critical to spend as much time as possible in the second space and as little as possible in the first.

These observations highlight the weakness of subjective well-being as a metric of welfare. The fact that people adapt quickly to new circumstances, good or bad, is a design feature of the brain's motivational system. The fact that a paraplegic may continue to be happy does not imply that his condition has not reduced his welfare. Indeed, many well-adjusted paraplegics report that they would undergo surgery entailing substantial risk of death to restore their mobility. Similarly, the fact that people may adapt quickly to higher income says nothing about whether economic growth makes them better off.

Critics of economic growth cite its threat to the planet's survival. Yet it is not growth per se that threatens but certain kinds of growth. Driving more SUVs causes harm, but taking more piano lessons does not. Any country with a government not beholden to corporate interests could easily curb environmentally harmful activities through taxation and regulation, redirecting spending toward things that really matter. Across developed countries, higher growth rates are actually associated with cleaner environments, not dirtier ones. The United States is the world's largest emitter of greenhouse gases not because of its wealth but in spite of it.

Environmentally sustainable economic growth promises to increase human welfare in a host of other important ways. For example, as the economist Benjamin Friedman reports in his book *The Moral Consequences of Economic Growth* (2005), societies in which incomes are growing more rapidly tend to support their poorest members more generously. Growth will support continuing investment in workplace safety, preventing tens of thousands of serious injuries each year. And it will continue to free people to spend additional time with their families.

But growth's most compelling promise is continuing progress against premature death, perhaps the most devastating of life's tragedies. American families with five children in 1800 often saw two or three of them die before the age of ten. That this no longer happens represents a landmark achievement.

Intelligently managed growth will hasten our quest to defeat diseases that continue to strike people down in the prime of life. The mere fact that rising incomes do not bolster self-assessed happiness levels is no reason to abandon this quest.

WHAT we measure influences what we do. In education, for example, critics of the No Child Left Behind Act offer evidence that focusing on standardized test scores causes teachers to neglect other important skills that are less easily measured. In the following selection, I argue that our single-minded focus on gross national product as a measure of economic success leads to similar problems.

15. Is GDP a Reasonable Measure of Economic Welfare?

Gross domestic product (GDP) is the most widely used measure of economic progress. Countries in which GDP is rising rapidly are viewed as economically successful, while those with stagnant GDP are seen as failures.

This traditional view has long been contested. Although everyone concedes that income is an imperfect welfare measure, conservative economists have tended to emphasize its virtues while liberals have been more likely to stress its shortcomings.

The debate is not just of philosophical interest; it also has important policy implications. Recent research findings offer support for specific arguments on both sides. Mounting evidence suggests, however, that per capita income is a less reliable measure of well-being when income inequality is rising rapidly, as in recent decades.

How do economists measure income? The most commonly used metric is gross domestic product, the annual market value of all final goods and services produced within a country. Per capita GDP is simply GDP divided by total population. Measured in 2000 dollars, it was $32,833 in 1998 and $37,832 in 2006. The real value of goods and services bought by Americans in 2006 was thus about 15 percent higher than it was in 1998. In purely economic terms, does that mean we were roughly 15 percent better off in 2006?

Not necessarily. To measure changes in the standard of living over time, it is necessary to adjust for inflation. But as conservatives stress, traditional inflation adjustments may overstate actual inflation because they fail to account adequately for quality improvements.

For example, although the current Honda Civic, a compact car, is about the same size as the company's midsize Accord from 1998, it is far superior and sells for only slightly more than the earlier Accord. Because inflation adjustments for auto prices are based on changes for corresponding models, the result is to overstate increases in owner- ship costs, thereby causing per capita GDP to understate the corre- sponding increases in our standard of living.

Quality changes are not always positive, by the way. If you had a question about your health insurance in 1998, you could talk to a real person; today, you may find yourself in an endless phone loop. On bal- ance, however, most consumers would probably prefer today's overall menu of goods and services in the economy to that of a decade ago.

Inflation adjustments may introduce further bias if people re- arrange their spending patterns when prices rise unevenly. When beef prices rise twice as fast as chicken prices, people typically eat less beef and more chicken. Traditional inflation measures fail to take such ad- justments fully into account, again, causing per capita GDP growth to understate increases in the standard of living.

Liberals have long objected that many expenditures included in GDP reflect reductions, not increases, in our standard of living. When crime rates increase, people spend more on burglar alarms, purchases that do not signal improved living standards. A similar ob- jection applies when tasks once performed at home are now bought in the marketplace, as when time-pressed parents substitute meals at fast food restaurants for home-cooked meals.

The bias that results from the inclusion of such expenditures in GDP works in the opposite direction from the bias caused by inaccu- rate inflation adjustment. For all anyone knows, the two distortions may roughly offset each other.

But there is a much bigger problem, one that challenges the very foundation of the presumed link between per capita GDP and eco- nomic welfare. That's the assumption, traditional in economic models, that absolute income levels are the primary determinant of individual well-being.

This assumption is contradicted by consistent survey findings that when everyone's income grows at about the same rate, average levels of happiness remain the same. Yet at any given moment, wealthy people are happier, on average, than poor people. Together, these findings suggest that relative income is a better predictor of well-being than absolute income.

In the three decades after World War II, the relationship between well-being and income distribution was not a big issue, because incomes were growing at about the same rate for all income groups. Since the mid-1970s, however, income growth has been confined almost entirely to top earners. Changes in per capita GDP, which track only changes in average income, are silent about the effects of this shift.

When measuring the economic welfare of the typical family, the natural focus is on median, or 50th percentile, family earnings. Per capita GDP has grown by more than 85 percent since 1973, while median family earnings have grown by less than one-fifth that amount. Changing patterns of income growth have thus caused per capita GDP growth to vastly overstate the increase in the typical family's standard of living during the past three decades.

Some economists have advanced an even stronger claim—that there is no link, at least in developed countries, between absolute spending and well-being. Recent work suggests that this is especially true for spending categories in which the link between well-being and relative consumption is strongest. For instance, when the rich spend more on larger mansions or more elaborate coming-of-age parties for their children, the apparent effect is merely to redefine what counts as adequate.

Evidence also suggests that higher spending at the top instigates expenditure cascades that pressure middle-income families to spend in mutually offsetting ways. Thus when all applicants spend more on interview suits, the same jobs go to the same applicants as before.

Yet in many other categories, greater levels of absolute income clearly promote well-being, even in the richest societies. The economist Benjamin Friedman has found that higher rates of GDP growth are associated with increased levels of social tolerance and public support for the economically disadvantaged. Richer countries also typically have cleaner environments and healthier populations.

That per capita GDP is an imperfect index of economic welfare is not news. The lesson of recent work is that its weaknesses are more serious than we previously realized.

And it is an especially uninformative metric when income inequality has been rising sharply, as it has been in recent decades. A society that aspires to improve needs a better measure of what counts as progress.

New York Times, March 9, 2008

IN the next selection, written in the summer of 1999, I explore the implications of the income-happiness nexus for tax policy. Are people happier when they get to keep the largest possible fraction of their pretax income to spend as they please? According to antigovernment conservatives, the answer is so obviously yes that it's almost pointless to pose the question. According to the best available evidence, however, it is far from clear that starving the public sector creates the greatest happiness for the greatest number.

16. Which Do We Need: Bigger Cars or Better Schools?

Tax cutters claim the moral high ground. "It's a matter of principle," says Bill Archer, chairman of the House Ways and Means Committee, "to return excess tax money in Washington to the families and workers who sent it here."

In pushing the current tax cut measures through Congress, Archer and other proponents have built their case on the proposition

that money spent in the private sector is almost always used more re-
sponsibly than money spent by bureaucrats.

At first glance, this appears unassailable. The Pentagon's $7,600
coffee maker may have been an aberration, but private fire companies
routinely deliver comparable protection at half the cost of their mu-
nicipal counterparts.

Adding to the appeal of tax cuts is that, despite our robust economy, millions of taxpayers feel strapped for cash. As a nation, we're
currently spending 1.2 percent more than we earn, and more than one
family in seventy filed for bankruptcy last year.

Yet the gains promised by tax cutters are illusory. A cut would
worsen an already serious imbalance in the overall mix of things
we buy.

A disproportionate share of the tax relief now being considered—
45 percent under the House plan and 30 percent under the plan the
Senate passed yesterday—would go to the wealthiest 1 percent of
households, which earn more than $300,000 a year. These households
have captured most of the growth in earned income during the past
twenty-five years, and their spending on luxury goods is already
growing at record rates.

With more cash in their pockets, top earners would demand still
bigger houses and cars. A sport utility vehicle just one inch wider than
Ford's new Excursion—which weighs three times as much as a Honda
Civic—would require special wide load running lights. And increased
spending at the top always spawns additional spending by others.

Ardent tax cut proponents will respond, "So what? If top earners
want to spend the wealth they have generated on bigger houses and
cars, why should Congress second-guess them? And if middle-class
families can't afford to keep up, why can't they just summon the will
to live within their means?"

But the problem confronting a family is like the one confronting a
participant in a military arms race. It can choose how much of its own
money to spend, but it cannot choose how much others spend. A
middle-income family that buys a smaller than average house typically

must send its children to below-average schools. Buying a smaller than average vehicle means greater risk of dying in an accident. Spending less—on bombs or on personal consumption—frees up money for other pressing uses, but only if everyone does it.

The persistent budget deficits of the past three decades have gutted many public services once considered essential. At a time when we are wealthier than ever, does it really make sense to be closing our public libraries on Sundays or cutting federal inspection of meat processing plants? Does it make sense not to replace antiquated water supply systems that deliver potentially dangerous levels of toxic metals, pesticides, and parasites to some 45 million of us?

Paradoxically, a tax cut could actually leave Americans with less to spend on themselves. Money spent on a tax cut instead of repairing a road means not only having to spend two to five times as much to fix that same road in the near future, but also having to pay an average of $120 per car to repair the damage that bad roads inflict each year.

·Proponents of smaller government argue that if we let the government spend more money, more will be wasted.

This is true, of course, but only in the trivial sense that there would be more of everything the government does—good and bad—if public spending were higher.

The solution favored by many opponents of government waste, epitomized in the Proposition 13 movement in California, is to starve the government.

But as Californians have belatedly recognized, this remedy is like trying to starve a tapeworm by not eating. Residents of the Golden State, who once proudly sent their children to the nation's best schools, are now sending them to some of its worst.

The question, then, isn't whether bureaucrats know best how to spend our money, but how much of our money we want to spend on public services.

The current budget surplus could be used to help restore public services that deliver good value for our money. Or it could be used to pay for tax cuts that would help fuel an already intense consumption spiral. Tired slogans about government waste won't help us make this decision more intelligently.

EVERY December, the *New York Times* arts and ideas editor asks a motley collection of contributors to identify the year's most overrated and underrated ideas. My earlier column on repeal of the estate tax (Chapter 1) grew out of my contribution to the list of most overrated ideas of 2003. This chapter's final selection was my contribution to that year's most underrated list.

17. Why Is Money Often Underrated?

Psychologists report that measures of human happiness scarcely change when national income grows. Citing this finding, many social critics now insist that income growth no longer promotes well-being.

Experience suggests otherwise. Years ago, when I was a graduate student with two children in diapers, my wife called in distress to report that our ten-year-old clothes dryer had died. That evening, I scanned the classified ads, made numerous calls, and the next day drove out to inspect several machines. After haggling with the owner of a five-year-old Kenmore, I wrote a check we could barely cover. I drove a friend's truck across town to pick it up, then drove twenty-five miles to take the old machine to the dump. Four days and numerous hardware store visits later, we again had a working dryer.

I now earn more than ten times what I did then. Recently my wife called to say that another dryer had died. "Call Werninck's," I suggested. When I got home that evening, the old machine was gone and a new one up and running.

Money doesn't guarantee happiness. But having enough can make life much less stressful.

4

Trailblazers

Cornell psychologist Tom Gilovich has shown that most people are surprised by someone they meet face-to-face after hearing stories about that person. Gilovich argues that when we describe someone, we tend to exaggerate distinctive or unusual traits. These descriptions are not incorrect, but are misleading because they are one-sided. The person we meet almost always seems less extreme, more nearly normal than the person we expected.

Something similar happens when a famous person retires, dies, wins an award, or experiences some other important transition. The expert commentators who assess the significance of that person's work in the aftermath of such transitions naturally highlight its most distinctive or extreme aspects. As a result, those with firsthand knowledge of the work often find these summaries misleading. I've often had this reaction when reading accounts of the work of scholars I've admired.

Even so, I've always enjoyed reading these kinds of articles and often gain valuable insights from them. One of the things I've most enjoyed about writing a regular *New York Times* column is the opportunity to add my own opinions to the mix. In recent years, I've developed a growing interest in the sociology of knowledge, a field that investigates how social and cultural currents influence the transmission of ideas. In the columns selected for this chapter, I look back on four economists whose work I feel has been summarized in misleading ways.

THE occasion for writing three of the four columns was an important transition—a death in two cases, the receipt of a Nobel Prize in the other. But the scholar whose work prompted the first piece is still alive and well. He has not won the Nobel Prize or, to my knowledge, any other major academic award. But he helped advance an idea that I believe will be recognized someday as essential to our attempts to understand consumer behavior. His profound insights, which were once centrally featured on almost every syllabus, have all but disappeared from leading economics textbooks.

18. Why Did James Duesenberry Suddenly Disappear?

Unless you are a professional economist nearing retirement, the name James S. Duesenberry is probably unfamiliar. That is unsurprising, because he wrote primarily for academic audiences while on the Harvard economics faculty from 1946 to 1989.

What is surprising is that most academic economists under fifty have also never heard of Duesenberry. His theory of consumer behavior clearly outperforms the alternative theories that displaced it in the 1950s, a striking reversal of the usual pattern in which theories are displaced by alternatives that better explain the evidence. His disappearance from modern economics textbooks is an intriguing cautionary tale in the sociology of knowledge.

But it also has important practical implications. Unless we understand what drives consumption, which makes up two-thirds of total
economic activity, we cannot predict how people will respond to policy changes like tax cuts or Social Security privatization.

Any successful consumption theory must accommodate three basic patterns: the rich save at higher rates than the poor; national savings rates remain roughly constant as income grows; and national
consumption is more stable than national income over short periods.

The first two patterns appear contradictory: If the rich save at
higher rates, savings rates should rise over time as everyone becomes
richer. Yet this does not happen.

The poor save at lower rates, Duesenberry argued, because the
higher spending of others kindles aspirations they find difficult to
meet. Poverty is relative. This difficulty persists no matter how much
national income grows, and hence the failure of national savings rates
to rise over time.

To explain the short-run rigidity of consumption, Duesenberry
argued that families look not only to the living standards of others,
but also to their own past experience. The high standard enjoyed by a
formerly prosperous family thus constitutes a frame of reference that
makes cutbacks difficult, which helps explain why consumption levels change little during recessions.

Despite Duesenberry's apparent success, many economists felt uncomfortable with his relative income hypothesis, which to them
seemed more like sociology or psychology than economics. The profession was therefore immediately receptive to alternative theories
that sidestepped those disciplines. Foremost among them was Milton
Friedman's permanent income hypothesis, which still dominates research on spending.

Friedman argued that a family's current spending depends not on
its current income, but rather on its long-run average, or permanent,
income. Because economic theory predicts that people prefer steady
consumption paths to highly variable ones, Friedman argued that
people would smooth their spending, saving windfall income gains

and drawing down savings to cover windfall losses. Consumption should thus be more stable than income over short periods.

Friedman also argued that a family's savings rate should be independent of its income, leading him to predict the long-run stability of national savings rates.

Friedman dismissed the high savings rates of the rich as a statistical artifact. Because many of those with high measured incomes in any given year will have enjoyed positive windfalls, their permanent income will be lower, on average, than their measured income for that year. So if they save windfall gains, they will save a higher proportion of their measured income than of their permanent income. The converse holds for those with low measured income in any given year, who will have experienced a preponderance of windfall losses that year.

Although it is a tidy story, its fundamental premises are contradicted by the data. As numerous careful studies have shown, for example, savings rates rise sharply with permanent income. Friedman's defenders responded by arguing that rich consumers want to bequeath money to their children. But why should the poor lack this motive? Another problem is that people consume windfall income at almost the same rate as permanent income. To this, Friedman responded that consumers appear to have unexpectedly short planning horizons. If so, then consumption does not depend primarily on permanent income.

Strangest of all, Friedman's theory assumes that context has no effect on judgments about living standards. It predicts, for example, that an investment banker will remain satisfied with his twin-engine Cessna, even after discovering that his new summer neighbor commutes to Nantucket in a Gulfstream jet.

In light of abundant evidence that context matters, it seems fair to say that Duesenberry's theory rests on a more realistic model of human nature than Friedman's. It has also been more successful in tracking actual spending. And yet, as noted, it is no longer even mentioned in leading textbooks.

What is going on here? Psychologist Tom Gilovich has suggested that someone who wants to accept a hypothesis tends to ask, "Can I believe it?" In contrast, someone who wants to reject it tends to ask, "Must I believe it?" Most economists, it appears, just never wanted to believe the relative income hypothesis, perhaps because it suggests the possibility of wasteful spending races.

Whatever the reason for Duesenberry's disappearance, the profession's mood seems to be changing. Since the Nobel Prize in economics was awarded to a psychologist, Daniel Kahneman, in 2002, economists have been showing a new receptiveness to insights from other social sciences.

Duesenberry, now eighty-six, is alive and well in Cambridge, Massachusetts. His theory is ripe for a second look.

THE economists who have won the Nobel Prize have all been outstanding. But the insights of some have been far more important and enduring than those of others. Few economists would disagree with my view that William Vickrey was clearly in the first category. Vickrey won the Nobel Prize in economics in October 1996 at the age of eighty-two and died three days later. Because the Nobel is awarded only to living scholars, the selection committee came perilously close to missing this opportunity to honor one of the true giants of the profession.

Thomas Schelling is another of the profession's true giants. His work has had a more profound influence on my own thinking than that of any other economist. For reasons I and many of my colleagues still find difficult to fathom, the Nobel selection committee repeatedly passed him by. So I was thrilled by the committee's long overdue announcement in October 2005 that Schelling, then eighty-four, would share the 2005 prize with Robert Aumann. In the next column, which was prompted by that announcement, I argue that the committee failed to cite what I believe will come to be seen as Schelling's most important contribution.

19. Why Do Hockey Players Feel They Need Helmet Rules?

Left to their own devices, hockey players invariably skate without helmets. Yet when they vote in secret ballots, they almost always favor a rule requiring the gear. If this rule is such a good idea, why don't players just wear helmets on their own?

Thomas C. Schelling posed this question in his book *Micromotives and Macrobehavior* (1978). I had described Schelling, a professor emeritus at the University of Maryland, as the greatest living economist not to have received the Nobel Prize, a description rendered obsolete when he won it this month, jointly with Robert J. Aumann of the Hebrew University of Jerusalem.

Although the Nobel committee cited Schelling's 1960 book, *The Strategy of Conflict,* history will judge *Micromotives and Macrobehavior* as the more important work. The earlier book was justly praised for framing the debate about nuclear deterrence in the cold war, while many questions in the later book seemed almost pedestrian. Yet Schelling's answers transformed the way many economists think about the relationship between competition and social welfare.

Adam Smith's celebrated theory of the invisible hand is the idea that individual pursuit of self-interest promotes the greatest good for all. When reward depends primarily on absolute performance—the standard presumption in economics—individual choice does indeed turn out to be remarkably efficient. But when reward depends primarily on relative performance, as in hockey, the invisible hand breaks down. In such situations, unrestricted choices by rational individuals often yield results that no one favors.

To explain why, Schelling observed that by skating without a helmet, a player increases his team's odds of winning, perhaps because he can see and hear a little better, or more effectively intimidate opponents. The downside is that he also increases his odds of injury. If he values the higher odds of winning more than he values the extra safety, he will discard his helmet. Yet when others inevitably follow suit, the competitive balance is restored—everyone faces more risk and no one benefits. Hence the attraction of helmet rules.

As in hockey, many of the most important outcomes in life depend on relative position. Because a "good" school is an inescapably relative concept, each family's quest to provide a better education for its children has much in common with the athlete's quest for advantage. Families try to buy houses in the best school districts they can afford, yet when all families spend more, the result is merely to bid up the prices of those houses. Half of all children will still attend bottom-half schools.

Schelling's example thus suggests a radical new perspective on the various ways societies restrict individual choice. Consider the similarity between helmet rules and workplace safety regulations. Because riskier jobs pay higher wages, workers can gain advantage by accepting them. Just as unrestricted hockey players may feel compelled to discard their helmets, workers who are free to sell their safety may realize that unless they seize the higher wages, they will consign their children to inferior schools. In each case, limiting our options can prevent a mutually disadvantageous race to the bottom.

The logic of Schelling's example also challenges the cherished theory of revealed preference, which holds that we learn more about what people value by watching what they do than by listening to what they say.

If someone chooses a risky job paying $1,000 instead of a safer one paying $900, the theory concludes that he must value the extra safety at less than $100. Maybe, but only in the sense that a bareheaded hockey player reveals that he values winning above safety. In both cases, we may learn more about what people value by examining the rules they support than by studying their individual choices.

A similar interpretation applies to the Fair Labor Standards Act, which requires employers to pay overtime premiums for all hours worked in excess of forty. Free market economists often denounce this, noting that many workers would voluntarily work the longer hours that employers would have offered in the absence of premiums.

Yet here too the incentives confronting workers are much like those confronting hockey players.

Thus as Schelling's fellow Nobel laureate, George A. Akerlof, has written, individuals can often increase the odds of promotion by working longer hours, but when others follow suit, everyone's promotion prospects remain roughly as before. The result is often a rat race in which all must work until eight o'clock each evening merely to avoid falling behind.

Schelling is no fan of heavy-handed bureaucratic intervention. Still, as his examples make clear, there can be no presumption that the self-serving choices of rational individuals produce the greatest good for all.

The invisible hand assumes that reward depends only on absolute performance. The fact is that life is graded on the curve.

New York Times, October 27, 2005

UNFORTUNATELY the Nobel selection committee does not always come to its senses in time, which may explain why the late John Kenneth Galbraith never won the prize. The committee could have honored Galbraith for work in several different areas. For instance, it could have cited *The Great Crash of 1929,* his account of the financial meltdown that precipitated the Great Depression, which is ripe with insights relevant to the most recent financial crisis. Or it could have cited *The Affluent Society,* which chronicles the glaring contrast between public squalor and private affluence that grew so pronounced in the decades after its publication in 1956. In the next column, written in the wake of Galbraith's death in 2006, I speculate about why he never won the committee's favor.

20. Why Did Galbraith Never Win the Nobel Prize?

The Nobel award in economics is not given posthumously. So John Kenneth Galbraith, who died last month at ninety-seven, will never receive one. Yet Galbraith was the most widely read economist of the twentieth century and was considered one of the most influential.

There are, of course, many distinguished economists who never receive a Nobel. But the list of winners also includes some whose work has had little lasting impact. So, why did the Nobel committee pass on each of its 36 opportunities to select Mr. Galbraith?

In *The Affluent Society,* published in 1958, Galbraith argued that Americans would lead longer, more fulfilling lives if they spent less on private luxuries and more on their external environments. As he memorably put it, "The family which takes its mauve and cerise, air-conditioned, power-steered, and power-braked automobile out for a tour passes through cities that are badly paved, made hideous by litter, blighted buildings, billboards, and posts for wires that should long since have been put underground."

The standards that define luxury consumption have escalated considerably since he wrote those words. Yet with 40,000-square-foot mansions going up all around us even as our government tells us we cannot afford to inspect most of the cargo containers that enter our ports, his assessment still resonates. Why, then, wasn't his work more warmly received by his fellow economists?

A succinct answer was offered by Milton Friedman, one of the first Nobel laureates in economics and Galbraith's longtime friend and passionate intellectual adversary. Interviewed just after Galbraith's death, he characterized Galbraith's work as "not so much economics as it is sociology."

Although many economists shared Galbraith's skepticism about prevailing spending patterns, they were also skeptical of his explanation of the imbalance. According to standard economic models, consumers survey available goods, then select those that best suit their preferences. But in Galbraith's account, the arrow travels in reverse: firms first decide which goods are most convenient to produce, and then employ marketing wizardry to persuade consumers to buy them.

Most economists conceded that firms would gladly exploit consumers in this fashion if they could, yet most also doubted that firms had the power to do so in the long run. Galbraith's account, they felt, gave short shrift to the inventiveness of greedy rival capitalists.

His critics argued, for example, that if consumers were paying high prices for goods of little intrinsic value, there would be "cash on the table," the economist's metaphor for unexploited profit opportunities. Rivals could thus earn easy money by offering slightly cheaper and better products, in the process luring exploited customers away. After all, the same marketing prowess that enabled Galbraith's firms to bamboozle consumers should also enable rivals to attract consumers to better options.

Galbraith's critics had a point. Indeed, his explanation for society's spending imbalance suffered from the same deficiency that has plagued arguments of social critics on the left since Karl Marx. Because it implied that greedy capitalists were leaving cash on the table, most economists couldn't accept it. To this day, however, many remain equally skeptical of Milton Friedman's competing claim that unbridled market forces ensure optimal allocation of society's resources.

Galbraith studied at the University of California at Berkeley in the 1930s. Had he received his training decades later, he would have been better equipped to come up with explanations that might have satisfied his critics. For instance, modern game theory, a staple of current economics programs, shows why bad allocations often occur even in highly competitive markets in which consumers and firms are doing the best they can individually.

The most compelling examples of such inefficiencies entail applications of the familiar stadium metaphor, in which all stand to get a better view, only to discover that none see better than if all had remained seated. Thus, Galbraith might have argued, consumers buy more luxurious cars in the rational expectation that the cars will deliver more than enough extra satisfaction to justify the cost, only to discover that when others follow suit, the effect is merely to redefine what counts as luxury.

In response, Galbraith's critics might have asked, "Why don't consumers just buy cheaper cars and vote for higher taxes necessary to finance better schools and a cleaner, safer environment?" After all, sophisticated consumers should realize that since everyone else would also be paying higher taxes, the cheaper cars they would be constrained to buy in the high-tax climate would prove just as satisfying as the earlier, more expensive ones.

Psychologists sometimes describe economists who pose such questions as having "high IQ but no clue." One of the best-documented findings in behavioral economics, a new field at the intersection of psychology and economics, is that consumers are often not nearly as sophisticated as traditional economic models assume. Had Galbraith studied behavioral economics, he might have poked fun at his critics for suggesting that normal people give even fleeting thought to how their own frame of reference might be shifted by the spending of others.

Galbraith's arguments may have failed to win the approval of free market economists. Yet unlike many of his critics, he recognized a bad allocation of resources when he saw one. Nobel Prizes are sometimes awarded to scholars who are wrong for the right reasons, but almost never to those who are right for the wrong reasons.

New York Times, May 11, 2006

ALTHOUGH Milton Friedman remained a controversial figure throughout his lifetime, few economists would deny that he was one of the most influential economists of the twentieth century. And unlike the case of John Kenneth Galbraith, there was little chance that the Nobel selection committee would overlook Friedman's work. When the Nobel Prize was first awarded jointly to Jan Tinbergen and Ragnar Frisch in 1969, there were scores of plausible candidates who were considered almost equally deserving. Friedman, who won the prize in 1976, got there well ahead of most of them.

Many continue to interpret Friedman's longtime free market advocacy to mean that he was little concerned about issues like inequality and the well-being of the poor. But those who knew him best insist otherwise. In the last selection in this chapter, written just after Friedman's death in 2006, I explore his contribution to the design of the earned income tax credit, the most innovative and widely adopted antipoverty program in the world.

21. Was Milton Friedman Really a Bleeding Heart?

Milton Friedman, who died last week at ninety-four, was the patron saint of small-government conservatism. Conservatives who invoke his name in defense of Social Security privatization and other cutbacks in the social safety net may be surprised to learn that he was also the architect of the most successful social welfare program of all time.

Market forces can accomplish wonderful things, he realized, but they cannot ensure a distribution of income that enables all citizens to meet basic economic needs. His proposal, which he called the negative income tax, was to replace the multiplicity of existing welfare programs with a single cash transfer (say, $6,000) to every citizen. A family of four with no market income would thus receive an annual payment from the IRS of $24,000. For each dollar the family then earned, this payment would be reduced by some fraction, perhaps 50 percent. A family of four earning $12,000 a year, for example, would receive a net supplement of $18,000 (the initial $24,000 less the $6,000 tax on its earnings).

Friedman's proposal was motivated in part by his concern for the welfare of the least fortunate. But he was above all a pragmatist, and he emphasized the superiority of the negative income tax over conventional welfare programs on purely practical grounds. If the main problem of the poor is that they have too little money, he reasoned, the simplest and cheapest solution is to give them more. He saw no advantage in hiring armies of bureaucrats to dispense food stamps, energy stamps, day care stamps, and rent subsidies.

As always, Friedman's policy prescriptions were shaped by his desire to minimize adverse economic incentives, a feature that architects of earlier welfare programs had largely ignored. Those programs, each administered by a separate bureaucracy, typically reduced a family's benefits by some fraction of each increment in earned income. Rates of 50 percent were common, so a family participating in four separate programs might see its total benefits fall by $2 for each extra dollar it earned. No formal training in economics was necessary to see that working didn't pay. In contrast, someone who worked additional hours under Friedman's plan would always take home additional after-tax income.

The negative income tax was never adopted because of concern that a payment large enough to support an urban family of four might induce many to go on the dole. With a payment of $6,000 per person, for example, rural communes of thirty would have a pooled annual payment of $180,000, which they could supplement by growing vegetables and raising animals. Because these groups could live quite comfortably at taxpayer expense, there would be an eager audience for accounts of their doings on the nightly news. Political support for such a program would be difficult to sustain.

Instead, Congress adopted the earned income tax credit, essentially the same program except that only employed people received benefits. One of the few American welfare programs widely adopted in other countries, the earned income tax credit has proved far more efficient than conventional programs, just as Friedman predicted. Yet because it covers only those who work, it cannot be the sole weapon in society's antipoverty arsenal.

This month, economic populists like Jim Webb, Jon Tester, and others were elected to Congress on pledges to strengthen the social safety net. In pursuing this task, they should take seriously Milton Friedman's concern about incentives. How might they expand support for the unemployed without undermining work incentives?

One possibility is government-sponsored employment coupled with negative income tax payments that are too small to live on, even in large groups. Most low-income people would continue working for private employers, as they now do under the earned income tax credit. For others, government would stand as an employer of last resort. With adequate supervision and training, even the unskilled can perform many useful tasks. They can plant seedlings on eroding hillsides, for example, or remove graffiti from public spaces. They can transport the elderly and handicapped. Coupled with low negative income tax payments, wages from public service or private employment could lift everyone from poverty. This combination would provide no incentive to go on the dole.

Friedman, of course, would not have welcomed an expansion of the federal bureaucracy. But as his own observations about the provision of government services made clear, guaranteeing employment at low wages would require no such expansion. By inviting companies to bid for program contracts, government could harness market forces to control costs.

In the face of huge budget deficits, is such a program affordable? In a 1943 article, "The Spendings Tax as a Wartime Fiscal Measure," Friedman proposed a progressive consumption tax as the best source of revenue to meet critical national objectives. In addition to reporting their incomes to the IRS, people would also report their savings, as they do now for 401(k) plans. The difference between income and savings is annual consumption. That amount, less a standard deduction, would be taxed at progressive rates. High tax rates on consumption by the wealthy, Friedman argued, would generate additional revenue with minimal sacrifice. So if providing greater economic security for low- and middle-income families is an important national objective, as many voters seem to feel, there are ways to pay the bill.

By all accounts, Friedman was a generous and compassionate man, someone more keenly aware of good luck's contribution to individual prosperity than many of his disciples. Careful students of his work will be inspired not to dismantle the social safety net but to make it more effective.

New York Times, November 23, 2006

5

The Dismal State
of Economics Education

M edical students receive intensive, hands-on instruction in performing the services they'll deliver on becoming doctors. The
same is true of those who train for professions such as law,
accounting, and public administration.

But those who aspire to become college and university professors
generally receive no such instruction. Instead, their study focuses on
mastering the knowledge of their respective disciplines. Nowhere do
they receive instruction on how best to impart what they know about
their subject to the students who want to learn it. No one teaches
them to teach. On reflection, this strikes most observers as strange,
especially since we now know that the human brain is better able to
absorb new information in some forms than others.

I've been teaching introductory economics courses for almost
forty years, and I've noticed that the most common mistake we make
as teachers is attempting to tell our students too much. Learning

theorists tell us that new brain circuits are constructed most effectively through intense repetition. During a normal day, most living organisms confront more information than they can possibly absorb. Evolution's implicit rule of thumb for dealing with this problem apparently goes something like this: "If you encounter something only once, ignore it; but if you see it multiple times, lay down brain circuits for dealing with it." Similarly, a class is more likely to impart lasting knowledge if we focus on a few central ideas and encourage students to work with them actively and repeatedly.

THE selected columns in this chapter describe attempts I have made to exploit this insight in the context of introductory economics courses. In the first one, I describe innovations in foreign language teaching that may also be helpful in other disciplines.

22. Why Is Economics Teaching So Ineffective?

When I began teaching economics in the 1970s, I noticed that many people were disappointed when they learned what I did for a living. When I began asking why, many said something like this: "I took Econ 101 years ago, and there were all those horrible equations and graphs."

Their unpleasant memories were apparently justified. Studies have shown that when students are tested about their knowledge of basic economic principles six months after completing an introductory economics course, they score no better, on average, than those who never took the course.

In other sectors of the economy, such dismal performance might provoke malpractice suits. But in the university system, students and their parents put up with this situation year after year.

Why aren't introductory economics courses more effective? One possibility is that professors try to teach their students far too much. The typical course bombards students with hundreds of concepts, many of them embedded in complex equations and graphs. As the

Nobel laureate George J. Stigler wrote more than forty years ago, "The brief exposure to each of a vast array of techniques and problems leaves the student no basic economic logic with which to analyze the economic questions he will face as a citizen." The mathematical formalism that has become the hallmark of economic research has yielded deep insights, but it hasn't helped introductory students learn basic economic principles.

The good news is that an approach that has revolutionized the teaching of foreign languages promises similar gains in economics and other disciplines. I took four years of Spanish in high school but was hard-pressed to make myself understood when traveling in Spain. In those days, most language courses focused on arcane grammatical details, the functional equivalent of the technical material that often bedevils introductory economics students. Today, the best language programs try to mimic the organic process by which children learn their native language.

My first exposure to the new approach came during my Peace Corps training for teaching math and science in rural Nepal. We learned grammatically correct speech, but we were never taught any formal grammatical rules. Starting from scratch, we had to be able to teach in Nepali just thirteen weeks later. The language skills we acquired were fairly basic, but we made it.

Just as a few simple sentence patterns enable small children to express an amazing variety of thoughts, a few basic principles do much of the lifting in economics. Someone who focuses on these principles and applies them repeatedly in examples drawn from familiar contexts can master them easily in a single semester.

The form in which ideas are conveyed is important. Perhaps because our species evolved as storytellers, the human brain is innately receptive to information in narrative form. Years ago, I stumbled on an assignment that plays directly to this strength.

Twice during the semester, I ask students to pose an interesting question based on something they have personally observed or experienced. In no more than five hundred words, they must use basic economic principles to answer it. I call it the "economic naturalist" assignment, in the spirit of field biologists who use Darwinian principles to interpret the traits and behavior of living things.

A high proportion of my students' papers invoke the cost-benefit principle, which says that a rational person should take only those actions whose benefits exceed their costs. This principle can help explain otherwise mysterious patterns of government regulation. My former student Greg Balet asked, for example, why parents are required to strap toddlers into a safety seat for even a short drive to the grocery store, yet are permitted to fly from New York to Los Angeles with toddlers on their laps.

One answer might be that if a plane crashes, it won't much matter if toddlers are in safety seats. But Balet argued that because the real benefit of restraining devices in airplanes is preventing injuries caused by air turbulence, safety seats would be as useful in planes as in cars.

The explanation must lie on the cost side, he said. Once you've set up a child safety seat in your car, it costs nothing additional to use it. If you're on a full flight from New York to Los Angeles, however, you must buy an extra ticket, which might cost you $1,000.

Safety seats are thus more likely to pass the cost-benefit test in cars than in planes. (Economists have a simple response to those who object that cost should play no role in safety decisions: "Do you get your brakes checked on your way to work each morning?")

Basic economic principles are not rocket science. They are accessible even to children. Lance Knobel, for example, who writes the blog DavosNewbies.com, said that he'd been regaling his eleven-year-old son with economic naturalist puzzles at bedtime, "and he can't get enough of them."

Given the importance of the economic choices we confront, both as individuals and as a society, more effective economics training would yield enormous dividends. And in light of the low bar established by traditional courses, there seems little risk in trying something different.

New York Times, August 12, 2007

A PROVOCATIVE study suggests that introductory economics courses may actually leave students less able to answer basic questions than they were before taking the course. The authors of the study argue that part of the problem may be that the professors themselves never really mastered the principles they are attempting to teach. In the next selection, I explore this disturbing development.

23. Is the Opportunity Cost Concept Really That Hard to Master?

Many reasons have been suggested for why introductory economics instruction typically leaves no lasting trace on students. Perhaps the most important problem is that professors try to cover too much. PowerPoint slides and other forms of classroom technology enable professors to throw out a prodigious volume of material each hour. And when they cover a lot of material, they feel they've done a good job. But how much of this can their students absorb?

Another problem is that the introductory course is increasingly tailored not for the majority of students but for the negligible fraction who will go on to become professional economists. Such courses focus on the mathematical models that have become the cornerstone of modern economic theory. These models prove daunting for many students and leave them little time and energy to focus on how basic economic principles help explain everyday behavior.

But there is an even more troubling explanation for students' failure to learn fundamental economic concepts: many of their professors may have only a tenuous grasp of these concepts, since they too took encyclopedic introductory courses, followed by advanced courses that were even more technical.

Consider, for example, the cost-benefit principle, which says that an action should be taken only if its benefit is at least as great as its cost. Although this principle sounds disarmingly simple, many people fail to apply it correctly because they do not understand what constitutes a relevant cost. For instance, the true economic cost of at-tending a concert—its "opportunity cost"—includes not just the ex-plicit cost of the ticket but also the implicit value of other opportunities that must be forgone to attend the concert.

Virtually all economists consider opportunity cost a central con-cept. Yet a recent study by Paul J. Ferraro and Laura O. Taylor of Georgia State University suggests that most professional economists may not really understand it. At the 2005 annual meetings of the American Economic Association, the researchers asked almost two hundred professional economists to answer this question:

"You won a free ticket to see an Eric Clapton concert (which has no resale value). Bob Dylan is performing on the same night and is your next-best alternative activity. Tickets to see Dylan cost $40. On any given day, you would be willing to pay up to $50 to see Dylan. Assume there are no other costs of seeing either performer. Based on this information, what is the opportunity cost of seeing Eric Clapton? (a) $0, (b) $10, (c) $40, or (d) $50."

The opportunity cost of seeing Clapton is the total value of every-thing you must sacrifice to attend his concert, namely, the value to you of attending the Dylan concert. That value is $10—the difference be-tween the $50 that seeing his concert would be worth to you and the $40 you would have to pay for a ticket. So the unambiguously correct answer to the question is $10. Yet only 21.6 percent of the professional economists surveyed chose that answer, a smaller percentage than if they had chosen randomly.

Some economists who answered incorrectly complained that if people could apply the cost-benefit principle, it did not really matter if they knew the precise definition of opportunity cost. So the re-searchers asked another group of economists to answer an alternative version of the question in which the last sentence was revised to read this way: "What is the smallest amount that seeing Clapton would have to be worth to you to make his concert the better choice?" Again, the correct answer is $10, and although this time a larger per-centage got it right, a solid majority still chose incorrectly.

When they posed their original question to a large group of college students, the researchers found that exposure to introductory economics instruction was strikingly counterproductive. Among those who had taken a course in economics, only 7.4 percent answered correctly, compared with 17.2 percent of those who had never taken one.

Teaching students how to weigh costs and benefits intelligently should be one of the most important goals of introductory economics courses. The opportunity cost of trying to teach our students an encyclopedic list of technical topics, it seems, has been failure to achieve that goal. As Ferraro and Taylor put it in the subtitle to their paper, it is "a dismal performance from the dismal science."

New York Times, September 1, 2005

IN my 2007 book, *The Economic Naturalist*, I included more than one hundred of the best student examples submitted over the years in response to my economic naturalist writing assignment. In this chapter's final selection, I describe two of my favorites.

24. Why Do Brides Buy and Grooms Rent?

Why do the keypad buttons on drive-up cash machines have Braille dots? It is an interesting question, since the patrons of these machines are almost always drivers, none of whom are blind. The answer, according to my former student Bill Tjoa, is that ATM manufacturers make keypads with Braille dots for their walk-up machines anyway, and it is cheaper to make all machines the same way. The alternative, after all, would be to hold two separate inventories and make sure that each machine went to the right destination. If the Braille dots caused trouble for sighted users, the extra expense might be justified. But they do not.

Tjoa's question was the title of one of two short papers he submitted in response to the "economic naturalist" writing assignment for my introductory economics course. The specific assignment is "to use a principle, or principles, discussed in the course to pose and answer an interesting question about some pattern of events or behavior that you personally have observed."

"Your space limit is five hundred words," the assignment continues. "Many excellent papers are significantly shorter than that. Please do not lard your essay with complex terminology. Imagine yourself talking to a relative who has never had a course in economics. The best papers are ones that would be clearly intelligible to such a person, and typically these papers do not use any algebra or graphs."

Over the years, my students have posed and answered literally thousands of fascinating questions. My favorite was submitted by Jennifer Dulski, who asked, "Why do brides often spend thousands of dollars on wedding dresses they will never wear again, while grooms often rent cheap tuxedos, even though they will attend many formal social events in the future?"

Decades ago, when I first started teaching introductory economics, it never would have occurred to me to give an assignment like this. The idea grew out of my participation in an early pilot program in Writing in the Disciplines, a new pedagogical movement that promises to revolutionize the learning process at every level. The aim of the program, which was sponsored by the John S. and James L. Knight Foundation, was to encourage students to write about concepts they were grappling with in the various disciplines.

The initiative was inspired by the discovery that there is no better way to master an idea than to write about it. Although the human brain is remarkably flexible, learning theorists now recognize that it is better able to absorb information in some forms than others. Thus, according to the psychologist Jerome Bruner, children "turn things into stories, and when they try to make sense of their life they use the storied version of their experience as the basis for further reflection." He went on, "If they don't catch something in a narrative structure, it doesn't get remembered very well, and it doesn't seem to be accessible for further kinds of mulling over." Even well into adulthood, we find it easier to process information in narrative form than in more abstract forms like equations and graphs. Most effective of all are narratives that we construct ourselves.

The economic naturalist writing assignment plays to this strength. Learning economics is like learning a language. Real progress in both cases comes from speaking. The economic naturalist papers induce students to search out interesting economic stories in the world around them. When they find one, their first impulse is to tell others about it. They are also quick to recount interesting economic stories they hear from classmates. And with each retelling, they become more fluent in the underlying ideas.

Many students struggle to come up with an interesting question for their first paper. But by the time the second paper comes due, the more common difficulty is choosing which of several interesting questions to pursue.

The paper is not a complete substitute for the traditional syllabus, but the lasting impact of the course comes mainly from the papers. When students come back to visit during class reunions, the equations and graphs long since forgotten, we almost always end up talking about the questions they have posed and answered during the intervening years.

To answer her question about wedding dresses, Dulski argued that because most brides wish to make a fashion statement on their wedding day, a rental company would have to carry a huge stock of distinctive gowns, perhaps forty or fifty in each size. Each garment would thus be rented infrequently, perhaps just once every four or five years. So the company would have to charge a rental fee greater than the purchase price of the garment just to cover its costs. In contrast, because grooms are willing to settle for a standard style, a rental company can serve this market with an inventory of only two or three tuxedos in each size. Each suit can thus be rented several times a year, enabling a rental fee that is only a fraction of its purchase price.

Daniel Boorstin, the former Librarian of Congress, used to rise at five o'clock each morning and write for two hours before going into the office. "I write to discover what I think," he explained. "After all, the bars aren't open that early." Boorstin's morning sessions were even more valuable than he realized. Writing not only clarifies what you already know; it is also an astonishingly effective way to learn something new.

New York Times, September 29, 2005

6

Thinking About
Health Care

In 2000, Deborah Shank was seriously injured when a truck rammed the driver's side of her minivan. Shank, then a shelf stocker at a Walmart store in Cape Girardeau, Missouri, had recently qualified for the company's health plan, so most of her immediate hospital expenses were covered. But because she was left confined to a wheelchair with permanent brain damage, she required full-time nursing care. With the proceeds of a lawsuit against the company whose driver caused the accident, a court set up a $417,000 trust to help defray the cost of her care.

In 2007, however, another court ordered the family to reimburse Walmart for the $470,000 it had spent for Shank's medical care. The second court's ruling cited a clause in the company's health plan that gave it the right to recoup medical expenses if an injured employee collected damage payments in a lawsuit.

The practice of expense recovery has been defended on the grounds that it is unfair for someone to be reimbursed twice for the same medical expenses. The proceeds of Shank's lawsuit, however, were insufficient to cover even her nursing care, much less her original hospital expenses.

Alone among industrial nations, the United States does not provide universal health care for its citizens. Some 45 million Americans lack basic health coverage, and although uncovered patients can often receive treatment in hospital emergency rooms, their medical expenses remain a major cause of bankruptcy even for families like the Shanks, who had reason to believe they were adequately insured.

In the aftermath of World War II, the European social democracies constructed elaborate social safety nets for their citizens, which included universal health coverage and a generous public pension system. In contrast, the American social safety net was relegated to the corporate sector. This approach was essentially an accident, inspired by an unusually generous labor pact struck between General Motors and the United Auto Workers during the early days of the postwar boom.

With big American corporations largely insulated from foreign competition during that era, the system worked reasonably well. But as health care costs began to escalate and markets became increasingly exposed to competition from abroad, the profit margins needed to support the safety net started eroding. Many employers have responded by offering health coverage and other benefits to fewer and fewer employees. And some, like Walmart, have taken increasingly aggressive steps to limit reimbursements under the coverage they still provide.

Although there is broad agreement among policy analysts that the U.S. health care system needs an overhaul, specific policy proposals continue to be debated. The selections in this chapter address issues in that debate.

PERHAPS the most difficult ethical question confronting health care professionals is the level of care provided for terminally ill patients— scarce resources that could be used to meet many other pressing needs. And although it is tempting to say that everyone should enjoy un-limited access to health care services, some steps clearly deliver far too little value to justify their cost. Where should we draw the line? In the first selection in this chapter, written in early 2006, I argue that moral sentiments like empathy play an essential role in attempts to answer this question.

25. Is Humane Treatment a Basic Right?

"Do the poor deserve life support?" asks the economist Steven E. Landsburg in an article published under that title in Slate (www.slate .com/id/2133518/?nav=fo). Posing the question, "A woman who couldn't pay her bills is unplugged from her ventilator and dies. Is this wrong?" Landsburg invokes "economic considerations" to sug-gest that the answer is no.

Many commentators have attacked his argument as morally pre-posterous. Well, yes. But it is also economically preposterous. The two judgments are related.

Tirhas Habtegiris, a twenty-seven-year-old legal immigrant, lay dying of cancer in the Baylor Regional Medical Center in Plano, Texas, kept alive by a ventilator. Physicians offered no prospect for her recovery. She was hoping, however, to hang on until her mother could reach her bedside from Africa.

Habtegiris had little money and no health insurance. On Decem-ber 1, hospital authorities notified her brother that unless another hos-pital could be found to treat his sister, Baylor would be forced to discontinue care after ten days. But even with Baylor's assistance, the family was unable to find a willing hospital. True to its word, Baylor disconnected her ventilator on December 12, invoking a law signed in

1999 by George W. Bush, then governor of Texas. The law relieved doctors of an obligation to provide life-sustaining treatment ten days after giving formal notice that such treatment was found to be medically "inappropriate."

Unlike the comatose Terri Schiavo, Habtegiris was fully conscious and responsive when she was disconnected, according to her brother, and she tried to continue breathing. Her brother and several other family members have described the agonizing spectacle of her death by suffocation over the next sixteen minutes. Her mother never got there. (Baylor officials have said their decision had nothing to do with financial considerations.)

In Baylor's defense, Landsburg argues that Habtegiris's treatment would have failed the economist's basic cost-benefit test, which says that an action should be taken only if its benefit exceeds its cost. The cost of care is relatively easy to calculate, but measuring its benefit is more difficult, and here Landsburg stumbles.

In general, economists measure the benefit of an action as what its beneficiaries would be willing to pay to see it taken. To place a rough upper bound on the benefit of supporting Habtegiris, Landsburg asks us to imagine that before her illness, she had been given a choice between free ventilator insurance and $75 in cash (his illustrative estimate of the cost of providing a healthy young person with such insurance). He assumes, plausibly, that she would have chosen the cash. The implication, he believes, is that the benefit of extending Habtegiris's care must be less than its cost.

He is mistaken for multiple reasons. For one thing, he ignores the economically compelling reasons for having social safety nets in the first place. Even those who are not poor recognize that catastrophe is only one unlucky break away—losing one's job and health insurance, for example, or being stranded in a mountain blizzard and unable to afford a helicopter rescue. With such prospects in mind, most people favor collectively financed rescue efforts. That a poor person would not, or could not, buy private insurance against such contingencies is entirely beside the point.

Even more troubling, Landsburg ignores moral emotions like sympathy and empathy. As economists since Adam Smith have recognized, economic judgments are often tempered by these emotions. The upshot is that large numbers of people benefit when a patient in imminent mortal danger receives treatment. Had the opportunity presented itself, many would have eagerly contributed to Habtegiris's care. But organizing numerous individual private fund-raisers for such cases is impractical, so we empower government to step in when the need arises.

Landsburg's argument finesses the important distinction between a "statistical life" and an "identified life," concepts introduced by economist Thomas C. Schelling. Schelling observed the apparent paradox that communities often spend millions of dollars to save the life of a known victim (someone trapped in a mine, for example) yet may be unwilling to spend even $200,000 on a highway guardrail that would save an average of one life each year.

This disparity is not economically irrational, Schelling insisted, because the community values what it is buying differently in the two cases. It is one thing to risk one's own life on an unlikely automobile accident, but quite another to abandon a known victim in distress.

By offering a transparently unsound economic argument in defense of the Habtegiris decision, Landsburg unwittingly empowers those who wrongly insist that cost and benefit have no legitimate role in policy decisions about health and safety. Reducing the small risks we face every day is expensive, and the same money could be spent on other pressing needs. We cannot think intelligently about these decisions without weighing the relevant costs and benefits.

But using cost-benefit analysis does not make one a moral monster. In the wealthiest nation on earth, a genuine cost-benefit test would never dictate unplugging a fully conscious, responsive patient from life support against her objections. Landsburg's argument to the contrary is wrongheaded, not just morally but also economically.

THE next selection, written in February 2007, takes up the question of why the U.S. health care system delivers such poor service despite spending twice as much per capita as the health systems in many other countries.

26. Why Does the U.S. Health Care System Work So Poorly?

In his State of the Union address, President George W. Bush proposed tax cuts meant to make health insurance more affordable for the uninsured. The next day, Stephen Colbert had this to say on his show on Comedy Central: "It's so simple. Most people who can't afford health insurance also are too poor to owe taxes. But if you give them a deduction from the taxes they don't owe, they can use the money they're not getting back from what they haven't given to buy the health care they can't afford."

Just so. As health economists have long known, market incentives induce private insurers to spend vast sums to avoid people who may actually require health care. This problem is mitigated (though not eliminated) by employer-provided group policies. Because the Bush proposal would steer people toward individual policies, it would actually strengthen the incentive to shun unhealthy people. Such people can now keep their insurance by not changing jobs. But no private company would want them as individual policyholders at a price anyone could afford.

That Bush's proposal will not shrink the ranks of the uninsured is not its most serious problem. Far more troubling is its embrace of a system that spends more than twice as much on health care, on average, as the twenty-one countries in which life expectancy exceeds ours. American costs are so high in part because private insurance multiplies administrative expenses; currently about 31 percent of total outlays.

Most health economists agree that government-financed reimbursement is the only practical way to control these expenses, many

of them stemming from insurers' efforts to identify and avoid unhealthy people. Canada's single payer health system, which covers
everyone, spends less than 17 percent on administrative expenses.

Annual health spending in the United States currently exceeds
$2 trillion. A single payer system that did nothing more than reduce
administrative expenses to the levels of other countries would save
roughly $300 billion annually.

Some critics worry that expensive but ineffective medical interventions may proliferate if health care becomes a federal responsibility.
But Victor Fuchs, a respected health economist at Stanford University, and Dr. Ezekiel Emanuel, chairman of the Department of Clini-
cal Bioethics at the National Institutes of Health, have outlined a
single payer plan that would limit such interventions far more effectively than the current system does. (A copy of their plan is on the
links page of my website, www.robert-h-frank.com.)

If the single payer system embraced by virtually all other developed countries is clearly the best solution, why doesn't the United
States adopt it? Some analysts concede its merits, but characterize it as
either unaffordable or politically unrealistic. But why should a policy
that promises better results for less money be considered a nonstarter?

There are two obstacles, each of which could be overcome by intelligent political leadership. One is the additional tax revenue that
the single payer system would require—a tough political hurdle. Yet
how complicated would it be to explain to voters that because the single payer plan would reduce costs substantially, every additional tax
dollar would be offset by an even larger reduction in private insurance spending? Given that such a system is much cheaper overall,
calling it unaffordable makes no sense.

The second obstacle is opposition from private insurers, who
would be understandably reluctant to abandon multibillion-dollar
annual profit streams. Those who stand to lose from policy changes
always battle harder than those who stand to gain, an asymmetry that
is exaggerated when losses would be concentrated and gains diffuse.
So, yes, the insurance industry would resist bitterly.

But intelligent leadership could overcome that resistance. When a pie gets bigger, everyone can get a larger slice. Because moving to a single payer system would make the economic pie bigger, it should be possible for everyone, including the insurance industry, to come out ahead.

The first step is to acknowledge that insurance companies are not evil, that they invested in good faith under tax laws that favored employer-provided private health insurance. To put them out of business overnight would be unjust.

Even so, they are not entitled to a permanent license to operate a system that has become economically unsustainable. The move to a single payer plan would save far more than enough to compensate insurance companies for lost profits. Compensation for losses could start at 100 percent, then be gradually phased out as companies shifted investments elsewhere.

Selling this argument in an era of fifteen-second sound bites would be challenging but hardly impossible. Indeed, forceful advocacy of the single payer approach offers a golden opportunity for any serious presidential candidate. Voters are fed up with rising insurance costs and dwindling coverage. On the merits, single payer coverage is an unassailable solution to both problems. Its rationale is simple enough to articulate clearly during a long campaign. And if the proposal were devised so that everyone stood to win, corporate interests would have little reason to attack it.

Critics of the single payer plan have long railed against the specter of socialized medicine, suggesting that it means receiving medical treatment from government functionaries. Yet people who have experienced single payer coverage firsthand seem unconcerned. When one of my sons needed surgery for a broken arm during a sabbatical in Paris, for example, the medical system we encountered was just as professional as the American one and far less bureaucratic. And in France, which spends half as much on health care as the United States and has more doctors and hospital beds per capita, everyone is covered.

We live in challenging times. Does a candidate who can't persuade voters to embrace the single payer approach deserve to be president?

New York Times, February 15, 2007

BECAUSE of the federal government's failure to expand health coverage, individual states have begun to step in. Some problems are not best addressed at the state level, however. In the following selection, written in the spring of 2006, I explain why health care is one of them.

27. Should the States Tackle Health Care?

In manufacturing, it is said, the French copy no one and no one copies the French. A parallel statement may soon apply to central elements of American public policy. In most of the world, for example, the primary responsibility for ensuring access to health care, regulating environmental quality, and supporting basic scientific research is exercised by national governments. But in this country, these tasks are increasingly managed by state and even local governments.

Last week, for instance, Massachusetts became the first state to enact legislation trying to ensure that all its citizens have access to health care. At least nineteen other states considered legislation expanding health care coverage in 2005. In January, eight states adopted new rules from the California Air Resources Board calling for a 30 percent reduction in carbon dioxide emissions from cars and light trucks by 2016, a step that Governor George E. Pataki of New York has also pledged to take. And Maryland became the fifth state to authorize state spending for basic stem cell research.

In each case, there are compelling economic reasons for delegating the activities to national, rather than state or local, governments. Yet in each arena, the federal government has failed to act. It refuses to join international efforts to limit greenhouse gases. It makes further cuts in federal support for basic scientific research, even as the nation's share of world patents continues to decline. And about 46 million Americans currently lack any form of health insurance.

Although it is no mystery why states are beginning to take the lead in these domains, it is important to understand why the recently enacted programs are destined to fall far short of what could have been achieved at the federal level.

The explanation begins with the question of why we have multiple levels of government in the first place. Almost all of us are subject to taxation and regulation by governments at the local, state, and national level. Although multitiered government entails substantial redundancy and inefficiency, there are good economic reasons for it.

As economist Charles M. Tiebout explained in a seminal paper published in 1956, providing public services at the local level enables us to better achieve our desired mix of public and private consumption.

People who like lots of parkland, well-maintained roads, large police forces, and good schools can thus gather in high-tax communities that provide these amenities, while others can choose low-tax communities and spend more of their income on private consumption. Local government also minimizes the distance between citizens and the lawmakers who tax and regulate them.

But for some public services, like national defense, scale advantages rule out primary reliance on local government. Indeed, the fact that big countries can field more effective armies than small ones is the primary explanation for why large nations became the norm.

Scale advantages, however, do not explain why health care policy, environmental regulation, and support for basic scientific research are best delegated to the federal government. Rather, the problem is that in each of these instances, programs at the state and local levels create perverse economic incentives.

A case in point is a proposal recently discussed in Ithaca, New York, where I live. Activists in this progressive upstate community (sometimes called "the People's Republic of Ithaca") called for a local income tax to finance a single payer health care system for local residents. According to health policy experts, such a system would eliminate the substantial waste associated with attempts by insurance companies to limit authorized services and avoid covering people with chronic medical conditions.

Yet despite this advantage, a health system operated at the local level could never work. Because people are free to move, such a plan would attract uninsured people with chronic conditions from surrounding cities, substantially raising the program's cost. In turn, the need to raise income tax rates would induce many of the community's more affluent taxpayers to flee to neighboring cities. The resulting death spiral would quickly doom the program.

Like local borders, state borders are completely permeable. So, unless a large number of other states simultaneously enact comprehensive health care legislation of their own, the new Massachusetts program will confront the same problem.

State efforts to regulate greenhouse gases and support basic scientific research are problematic for a different reason. When a pound of carbon dioxide is emitted into the atmosphere, it quickly disperses around the globe. A state that regulates greenhouse gases thus bears the entire cost of the reduction but receives only a minuscule fraction of the benefit. That fact is bound to limit political support for curbs strong enough to matter. As economists have long emphasized, effective environmental regulation requires national or even international collective action.

It is the same with support for basic scientific research. Residents of Maryland will bear the entire cost of any discoveries from research they finance but will reap only a small fraction of the corresponding benefits. And because of that imbalance, their incentive will be to invest too little.

My point is not that states are foolish for extending their reach. Again, the federal government has completely dropped the ball in these domains. The recent state actions may not be the most efficient ways of dealing with our most pressing problems. But they send an unmistakable signal of voter impatience with ineffective government at the federal level.

New York Times, April 13, 2006

RECENT years have seen the emergence of boutique health care plans, as people of means pay as much as $20,000 a year in additional premiums in return for access to physicians with lighter case loads and hospital facilities offering monogrammed robes and heated towel racks. In the next selection, I argue that although the contrast between such plans and the care available to the uninsured may offend, moral outrage is better directed at other targets.

28. Is Boutique Health Care a Problem?

Although psychologists continue to quibble about the exact nature of the relationship between money and happiness, all available evidence suggests that the most well-to-do members of a community enjoy significantly higher levels of physical and psychological well-being than their economically less fortunate neighbors. As a wag once put it, those who insist that money doesn't buy happiness just don't know where to shop.

The recent emergence of boutique health plans provides yet another reminder of the advantages of wealth. By paying hefty fees above their normal health insurance premiums, subscribers can sidestep the most nettlesome frustrations of the managed care revolution, which has pressured doctors to cut costs by allocating less and less time to each patient visit. While a physician in a standard practice may care for thousands of patients each year, some new boutiques assign only three hundred, others as few as fifty, patients per doctor. Many of the new plans offer same-day appointments, on-demand cell phone access to doctors, and stand ready to shepherd patients through their dealings with specialists.

News of these luxury health plans has triggered the inevitable firestorm of protest from social critics. But these critics are barking up the wrong tree when they complain about the greed of physicians who offer the new plans and the selfishness of the patients who subscribe to them. In a free market economy, it is quixotic to expect people who can afford high-quality services not to demand them. And it is no sin to offer such services if you are talented enough to be chosen by the discerning buyers who seek them.

The real moral crisis in health care lies elsewhere. It is that more than 40 million Americans have no health insurance at all, and another 20 million are significantly underinsured.

Attempts during the Clinton administration to address this problem foundered because many feared that the Clinton proposal, which called for detailed federal regulation of the health care system, might create more difficulties than it eliminated. Yet universal access to the health care system can be provided by means of essentially the same nonbureaucratic mechanism that conservatives advocate so strongly in education: The federal government could simply grant each family— rich or poor—a voucher for purchasing a basic health care policy.

This solution would add to the federal budget, but it would also eliminate much of the egregious waste currently generated by a health care system that treats uninsured patients in costly emergency facilities and lets minor health problems grow into major ones. Under the voucher approach, people could choose their own health plan, totally free from meddling by the federal government.

Unfortunately, this solution is precluded in the near term by the president's statement that a tax increase will occur over his dead body. The Bush administration has been unwilling to consider the one budgetary step that would solve the health care access problem, and it has also pursued a fiscal agenda that is all but certain to make this problem worse.

Witness the $1.35 trillion tax cut enacted last year, most of it targeted for America's wealthiest families. The iron-clad economic rule is that as disposable incomes rise, families buy goods and services of higher quality. By putting hundreds of billions of dollars of additional purchasing power into the hands of wealthy families—already the only group to have enjoyed significant real income growth during recent decades—the tax cut will accelerate the new trend toward boutique medical practice. As each physician who joins one of these practices sheds a thousand or more patients, loads in the rest of the system will grow that much heavier.

The president sold his tax cuts on the slogan that "it's your money and you know how to spend it better than the Washington bureaucrats do." But as the events of September 11 have made clear, that slogan misses something important. Yes, it's our money, but we cannot achieve a healthy, secure society unless we spend it intelligently on public as well as private purposes.

Social critics correctly point out that there is something profoundly troubling about so many American families lacking access to even rudimentary medical care while others add $20,000 and more to their insurance premiums to enroll in plans that offer heated towel racks and individually monogrammed dressing gowns. But if there are culprits in this drama, they are neither wealthy patients nor the doctors who serve them. They are the legislators who supported the tax cuts that have made it impossible to address this problem.

Unpublished, 2002

IN this chapter's final selection, written during the closing months of the Clinton administration, I discuss the social forces that help explain why the number of people without employer-provided health insurance in the United States was growing so rapidly. My estimate of the cost of providing universal coverage seems quaint by today's standards, a measure of how rapidly health care costs have been rising in the interim.

29. Why Has the Number of Uninsured Risen So Sharply?

Last week we learned that poverty in the United States has been declining of late, but now we're told that the number of Americans without health insurance has risen to 44.3 million—833,000 more than a year ago and 4.5 million more than when Bill Clinton took office in 1993. Even in households with annual incomes of at least $50,000, the number of people without insurance increased last year to 12.2 million.

In the midst of the longest sustained economic boom in history, with the lowest unemployment rate in thirty years, how is it possible that the ranks of the uninsured keep swelling?

The simple answer is that millions of American families continue to experience day-to-day financial distress. Last year, for example, one of every sixty-eight families filed for bankruptcy, more than the number of families with children graduating from college.

Under the circumstances, it is easy to see why many families that enjoy good health are tempted to press their luck. After all, health coverage for a family of four with no preexisting medical conditions costs upward of $3,000 a year, which is almost always far more than what such a family spends on medical services. The extra cash could help pay for a move into a better school district, for example, or at least keep creditors at bay.

Of course, in the event of a catastrophic illness, the hoped-for savings would vanish, and then some. Yet many Americans ignore this possibility, having an unwarranted, even preposterous degree of optimism regarding their future well-being.

Surveys reveal that we see ourselves as far more likely than our peers to earn large salaries in the future, for example, and far less likely to get divorced or suffer from lung cancer. We may know that *some* families will have health problems, but we don't think we'll be among them.

As more people cancel their health coverage, going without insurance becomes more socially acceptable. Parents who didn't buy health insurance for their families were once viewed as irresponsible, but this stigma inevitably loses its sting as the number of uninsured grows.

Making matters worse is the changing composition of the pool of the insured. As more healthy families forgo coverage, those left tend to be sicker and more costly to treat, forcing up premiums.

A similar dynamic is at work on the employer's side. Not long ago, many workers would never have considered a job that didn't offer health insurance. As more employers, particularly small businesses, offer jobs with no coverage, however, it becomes more difficult for workers to avoid them. In turn, these employers have lower operating costs, allowing them a competitive edge and putting further pressure on businesses that continue to offer such benefits.

In short, our health insurance system is in a death spiral. Despite President Clinton's effort to expand coverage for uninsured children, we now have more uninsured children than ever. Vice President Al Gore's plan to broaden children's coverage is only a marginal improvement. Former senator Bill Bradley's proposal would substantially broaden coverage for both children and adults, but as even he concedes, it probably would not be enough. Governor George Bush has yet to weigh in on this issue.

The good news is that the government could eliminate the death spiral by simply reimbursing each family up to $3,000 a year for health insurance. Government bureaucrats would not need to prescribe which doctors we see or micromanage any of the other details. They would simply process insurance receipts and send out reimbursement checks.

This plan sounds expensive, but would actually be far less costly than the current system. The principal savings would come from delivering more cost-effective care to those who are now uninsured.

As it stands now, the untreated minor illnesses of the uninsured often develop into major illnesses, which are far more costly to treat.

And when such illnesses befall the uninsured, we almost always treat them, often in costly emergency rooms. The resulting burden on hospitals leads to higher fees and increased government support, both of which now come largely out of the pockets of high-income taxpayers with health insurance.

The total budget needed to finance a $3,000 health insurance reimbursement for every American family—some $200 billion a year—would obviously require higher taxes. But for those whose employers currently provide health insurance, these taxes would be offset by an increase in salaries.

After all, companies offer insurance not because they are charitable, but because they find doing so an effective way to compete for workers. Any company that did not offer higher salaries to previously insured workers would risk losing them to a company that did.

A universal reimbursement program would impose no net burden on taxpayers, because of both salary adjustments and reductions in the high cost of care for the uninsured. And by providing a powerful incentive for all families to buy insurance, it would reverse the current downward spiral.

Critics of health care reform will say that if some people want to save money by going without health insurance, that's their problem or their choice. Perhaps, but it's a problem for the rest of us as well, one that if left untended will grow steadily worse. Our unwillingness to deal with this problem is even more profoundly irrational than the uninsured family's belief in its immunity from serious illness.

New York Times, October 6, 1999

7

Getting
Prices Right

In my introductory economics course, I often ask students to imagine having a choice between two otherwise identical apartments. In one, their utilities are metered and billed separately, while in the other their utilities are included in the rent. I remind them that if they choose to have utilities included, the landlord will have to raise the rent by enough to cover the cost.

Most students initially prefer utilities included, yet most of them would be better off with separate metering and billing. When utilities are metered and billed separately, each tenant has an incentive to weigh the value of additional energy use against its cost when deciding whether to raise the thermostat setting or put on a sweater. Suppose, for example, that raising the setting from 65 to 70 degrees for the month of January would raise the monthly bill by $50. If the extra comfort is worth more than at least $50 to the tenant, he will raise the setting. But if it is worth less than $50, he'll leave the setting where it is.

In contrast, when utilities are included in the rent, the marginal charge facing each tenant for additional energy use is almost zero. For the example just considered, if any one tenant turned up his thermostat in a building with one hundred tenants, each tenant's share of the resulting $50 increase in the building's utility bill would be only fifty cents. The upshot is that it would be rational for an individual tenant to turn up the thermostat if the extra comfort was worth at least fifty cents. The problem is that if all tenants operate under the same incentive, all will turn their thermostat up, and their monthly bills would go up by $50 each. If the higher thermostat setting were actually worth only $20 a month to each tenant, each would be about $30 worse off each month when utilities were included.

This loss occurs because the artificially low energy price that tenants see when utilities are included in their rent encourages them to use energy wastefully. Once students have worked their way through numerous similar examples, most grasp the basic principle that people will waste valuable resources whenever they are permitted to purchase them at a price well below their actual cost.

By the time students complete my course, most will experience an instant skeptical reaction to any policy that tries to peg the price of a good or service at a level significantly different from the cost of producing the last unit (its "marginal cost," in the economist's shorthand). Whenever price is different from marginal cost, people will use the good or service wastefully. If price is set below marginal cost, they will use too much of it. And if price is set above marginal cost, they will use too little.

THE selections in this chapter focus on policies that attempt to peg prices at levels different from marginal cost. Such policies, I argue, are almost always misguided. When price is different from marginal cost, moving it closer to marginal cost will almost always enable us to make some people better off without harming others. Because this basic principle is not widely understood, however, policy makers are often reluctant to adopt marginal cost pricing. In the first selection in this chapter, written in March 2007, I consider the consequences of lawmakers' reluctance in the case of traffic congestion in New York City.

30. Why Is Congestion Pricing So Rarely Adopted?

New York City Mayor Michael R. Bloomberg recently proposed charging a fee to motorists who enter Manhattan south of 86th Street on weekdays. Car drivers would face a daily charge of $8 from 6:00 AM to 6:00 PM, while the fee would be $21 for commercial truck drivers.

Although critics have attacked the plan, experience suggests that the economic benefits of what is known as "congestion pricing" are substantial. For example, after a daily fee of $14 was imposed on cars entering central London in February 2003, downtown traffic fell by a third and travel times on some bus lines fell by half. Londoners also saw carbon dioxide emissions fall by 20 percent, and there were substantial declines as well in emissions of particulates and nitrogen oxides, the main components of smog.

But if the benefits of congestion pricing are so compelling, why is it so rarely adopted in this country? Perhaps the most important hurdle has been concern about hardships on low-income residents. For congestion fees to achieve their intended effects, they must be high enough to cause large numbers of people to alter their behavior. But fees that high would inevitably be burdensome for at least some people.

When this concern is not adequately addressed, proposals to change behavior by relying more heavily on market incentives are seldom accepted. Although studies have shown, for example, that daily and seasonal variations in electric rates would substantially reduce the average consumer's utility bills, proposals to adopt such rate plans are typically rejected because of concerns about low-income users who may lack the flexibility to alter their consumption patterns.

That such concerns often block economically efficient programs is one of the enduring mysteries of modern political economy. An economically efficient program is, by definition, one whose benefit exceeds its cost. That means there must be ways of redistributing the gains so that every citizen, rich and poor, comes out ahead. Failure to adopt an efficient program thus raises the question of why we couldn't figure out how to accomplish the necessary transfers. Why are we leaving cash on the table?

It is already clear that concerns about the effect of congestion fees on poor motorists underlie much of the gathering opposition to the mayor's plan. Lewis A. Fidler, a New York City councilman, for example, has called the plan "outrageous, because they're saying rich people can come into Manhattan and poor people may not, and that is just wrong, wrong, wrong." Unless such concerns can be satisfactorily addressed, they are likely to sink the mayor's proposal.

Mayor Bloomberg would do well to study the New York State Public Service Commission's attempt to impose fees for directory assistance in the mid-1970s. That experience illustrates not only the decisive importance of equity concerns in public policy decisions, but also how easy it often is to address them.

In a reform effort begun by Joseph C. Swidler, then the chairman, and completed by his successor, Alfred E. Kahn, the agency that regulates New York's public utilities took aim at the now quaint-seeming practice of providing directory assistance free. The commission argued that a ten cent charge for directory assistance calls would give consumers an incentive to look up telephone numbers on their own whenever convenient, which would free up operators and equipment for more valuable tasks.

Although the commission's proposal promised net benefits for the average telephone subscriber, it was greeted by a firestorm of protest. And when social scientists testified gravely, albeit absurdly, that it threatened to disrupt vital networks of communication in the community, its defeat appeared certain.

Commission officials then introduced a simple amendment that saved it. In addition to charging ten cents for each directory assistance call, they proposed a thirty cent credit on each consumer's monthly phone bill, a reduction made possible by the additional revenue from the charge and the savings from reduced volumes of directory assistance calls. Because this amendment promised to reduce the monthly bill of customers willing to use their phone books, political opposition vanished overnight.

No one who witnessed this episode came away without a deep appreciation of how strongly the fate of public policy proposals is tied to concerns about how they will affect the poor. After all, those concerns nearly defeated an otherwise unimpeachable proposal, even though a ten cent charge for directory assistance calls would have had essentially no impact on even the poorest family's standard of living.

If Mayor Bloomberg wants New Yorkers to reap the considerable benefits promised by congestion pricing, he should follow the Public Service Commission's example. Although most people who currently commute by car into Manhattan are not poor, some are, and for these drivers, paying $8 each day would be difficult. It is an iron law of politics that those who stand to lose from a change in policy lobby much more intensively than those who stand to benefit. Rather than allow concern for poor drivers to doom congestion fees, the city should adopt a simple variant of the phone bill rebate.

For example, every worker in Manhattan could be given transferable vouchers that could be used to defray some portion of the new fees. This would protect low-income people who sometimes have no choice but to drive into the city during peak hours. Those who could avoid such trips could sell some or all of their vouchers to others. All New Yorkers could thus enjoy the benefits of cleaner air and reduced traffic congestion without imposing a burden on low-income families.

Can the city afford to address concerns about low-income motorists in this way? With New York's rapidly growing population making congestion more severe each year, a better question may be whether it can afford not to.

New York Times, March 10, 2007

RELUCTANCE to adopt congestion pricing is by no means limited to the public sector. When the management of the New York Mets baseball team first proposed setting higher prices for the games in highest demand, many fans objected that the practice was unfair. But as I argue in the next selection, written just after the Mets first proposed their new pricing scheme in late 2002, charging more for more heavily attended games is actually a fairer way of apportioning the organization's costs among different fans.

31. Why Do Prices Generally Vary Too Little?

The management of the New York Mets baseball team adopted variable ticket pricing in the spring of 2003 because Shea Stadium is like a commercial airliner. When a 757 takes off from nearby LaGuardia Airport with unfilled seats, something of value is lost forever: the airline loses the revenue, and passengers lose the chance to travel. When the Mets play before less than sellout crowds at Shea, both the team and its fans lose as well.

Airlines have long used sophisticated pricing methods to fill empty seats, and the Mets' move follows a similar logic. Prior to 2003, a given seat at Shea sold for the same price every day. Seats now sell at four different prices, depending on when the game occurs and the popularity of the opposing team. In the 2002 season, fans could catch the lowly Brewers on a May weekday for as little as $8, down from $12 in 2002. But to see Barry Bonds hit a home run on a July Saturday in 2003, they had to pay at least $16.

Economic theory's ideal pricing scheme is one that eliminates excess demand during peak periods while serving customers at cost during off-peak periods. By that standard, the Mets' move is a clear improvement. Of course, that fact hasn't prevented the inevitable complaints about higher prices for popular games. The real problem, however, is that the new formula doesn't go far enough. Saturday Yankees games in July still sell out months in advance, and Monday Brewers games in May still fill less than a third of Shea's seats.

The Mets are not unique in departing from the economist's ideal price structure. Why do so many hotels, restaurants, and other businesses charge prices that are too low when they're busy and too high when they're not? Their concern is that aggressive peak period pricing might court a customer backlash. Why go to a restaurant that charges double on Saturdays, angry customers might wonder, even though the meal costs no more to prepare than on other nights?

This question betrays a faulty understanding of cost. Although the raw ingredients cost no more on Saturdays, the cost of serving additional diners is still far greater than on other days, because the restaurant would have to enlarge its facilities and buy more equipment to accommodate larger crowds. Additional Tuesday patrons, in contrast, can be served without spending an extra cent on such items. A similar logic applies to the Mets, who would need a bigger stadium and more parking to serve additional fans at sellouts.

Would larger price differentials be fair? Customers don't feel betrayed when grocers charge them three times as much for three pounds of beef as for one pound, since those who buy more obviously impose higher costs on the seller. By the same token, peak period users of stadiums or restaurants should pay higher prices, because they too impose higher costs. But because the cost differences in these cases are less obvious, customers often regard price differentials as unfair. This perception is an illusion.

No strategy will fill more empty seats at Shea than for the team's new manager to guide the Mets to a winning season. By all means, let the quest to win continue. Meanwhile, the team and its fans will gain by having prices that track costs more closely.

IN the summer of 1978, I left my teaching position at Cornell to serve for the next two years as chief economist for the Civil Aeronautics Board in Washington, D.C. The CAB, now defunct, had just launched the process of deregulating the nation's commercial air transport system under the leadership of its chairman, Alfred Kahn.

With deregulation came substantial fare reductions and increases in traffic, much to the delight of the traveling public. Over time, however, increased traffic led to increased congestion and delays. Many travelers now seem to believe air transport deregulation may have gone too far. In the following selection, I argue that the reverse is true. Much of the congestion that chokes the current system is the result of the Federal Aviation Administration's failure to charge airlines prices that reflect the market value of landing and takeoff rights at the nation's most congested airports.

32. Why Should Travelers Get a Valuable Resource for Free?

In April 2000, Congress passed a law intended to stimulate competition at La Guardia Airport and increase service to small communities. In response, the Federal Aviation Administration substantially increased the number of flights allowed to operate at La Guardia, already one of the nation's busiest airports.

But La Guardia couldn't handle the new traffic, and a week ago the FAA rolled back the number of daily flights to pre-April levels. Then it held a lottery for operating slots that gave preference to nine small airlines.

Reducing operating slots in this way clearly ameliorates crowding. But it does so in a wasteful way that guarantees continued unfairness and frustration for area travelers.

Slots at crowded airports are a valuable economic resource, much like scarce seats on an oversold flight. History has taught us a valuable lesson about how best to allocate seats on oversold flights, one with a message for the problem of crowded airports.

Carriers once handled oversold flights on a first-come, first-served basis. If 120 passengers presented tickets for a flight with 100 seats, only the first 100 got to go. For passengers coming from connecting flights, this was like a lottery. If your connecting flight was late, you got bumped.

This solution never considered that individuals have different needs. People with urgent schedules were often forced to wait, while those less pressed made their flights.

Parallel issues arise with overcrowded airports. Just as a plane can accommodate only so many passengers, an airport can handle only so many operations. So every time a nineteen-seat Beechcraft 1900 uses La Guardia, the FAA must deny permission to some larger plane, say, a Boeing 757 with several hundred passengers. Today, even among carriers currently authorized to use La Guardia, delays and flight cancellations are legion. More important, a host of carriers would like to provide large aircraft service to La Guardia but are not authorized to use the airport at all. That means some travelers have to use less convenient airports, just as someone has to wait when flights are oversold. In both cases we have a strong interest in minimizing total inconvenience.

On this score, the La Guardia lottery is even worse than first-come, first-served. Not only does it make no attempt to minimize the number of diverted passengers, but it actively increases their number by setting aside special slot allocations for carriers that serve small communities with small aircraft.

There are better ways to solve both problems. In 1979 the Civil Aeronautics Board called for carriers to offer cash payments, free tickets, or other rewards to induce volunteers to relinquish their seats on oversold flights. Passengers could decide for themselves how important it was to avoid waiting. Those with pressing business simply wouldn't volunteer. The board's proposal was adopted and became widely recognized as both more fair and more efficient than the earlier system.

Scarce operating slots at La Guardia can be allocated in essentially the same way. Rather than give them away by lottery, the FAA could sell them to the highest-bidding airlines. If the market value of a slot were, say, $5,000, carriers would have to charge travelers on a twenty-passenger flight $250 more for a one-way ticket, while those on a two-hundred-passenger flight would have to pay only $25 extra. Passengers on small flights would thus have a strong incentive to divert to less crowded times or less crowded airports.

For oversold flights, the auction solution works because it gives people an incentive not to use a scarce seat unless its value is high to them. Similarly, auctioning operating slots at crowded airports creates an incentive to use those airports only if the value of doing so is high.

Granted, this doesn't do much for passengers from Ames, Iowa, who want to visit New York City. But they can still fly to nearby airports, especially in Westchester or Long Island. And if aviation authorities really wanted to help the citizens of small communities, they could sell scarce slots to the highest bidders, then give cash compensation to those communities that suffered as a result.

Even if such compensation is impractical, we should bite the bullet and realize that the best way of minimizing the inconvenience we impose on air travelers is to charge handsomely for the convenience of landing at La Guardia.

New York Times, December 13, 2000

IN this chapter's final selection, I explain why taxes are sometimes the easiest way of pushing the price of a good closer to its true marginal cost. This column was written in the spring of 2000, shortly after a *Wall Street Journal* report suggested that SUVs, by virtue of their higher mass, are safer than passenger sedans. Two years later, Keith Bradsher argued in his book *High and Mighty* that SUVs are in fact safer only in head-on collisions. Because of their increased vulnerability to rollovers, SUV drivers are actually more likely to be injured or killed in accidents than the drivers of cars. But regardless of whether SUVs are safer than cars, their mass clearly creates additional risk of injury and death to other drivers. And that fact justifies additional taxes on them.

33. If SUVs Put Others in Danger, Why Not Tax Them?

Each year for the past decade, the automaker that has offered the biggest lineup of heavyweight sport utility vehicles has won a huge sales and profit windfall. SUVs now account for some 20 percent of all vehicles sold by Ford (up from 5 percent in 1990), and brisk sales of the company's massive new Excursion have been generating profits of roughly $18,000 per vehicle, several times the margin for passenger cars.

By one recent estimate, the Excursion and other jumbo vehicles accounted for most of Ford's record profit of $7.2 billion last year.

Now William Clay Ford Jr., the company's chairman and the great-grandson of founder Henry Ford, has begun to voice second thoughts. An ardent environmentalist, he concedes that the Excursion's fuel consumption (10 miles per gallon in the city, 13 on the highway) helps worsen global warming, and that its bulk (more than 7,500 pounds, three times as heavy as a Honda Civic) puts other motorists at risk.

With environmentalists deriding his company's new profit leader as the "Ford Valdez," Ford understandably feels a twinge of conscience.

But has he really done anything wrong? Consumers have voted with their dollars that they want larger vehicles, and if Ford had not supplied them, some other company surely would have.

Sticking to small vehicles might have soothed Ford's feelings but would have been a disaster for his shareholders.

It might seem that the real blame, if any, lies with consumers. But on closer inspection, it is hard to find fault with people who are simply trying to protect their families from being killed in auto accidents. The simple fact is that bigger means safer.

A recent *Wall Street Journal* study, for example, found that the five safest vehicles on the road today are sport utility vehicles (average weight: 5,500 pounds, not including the Excursion, whose weight was unavailable for the study). Among the fifty vehicles identified as safest by the *Journal* study, eighteen were SUVs, twenty-three were large pickup trucks or vans, and only nine were passenger sedans (large ones like the 4,100-pound Lincoln Town Car, also by Ford).

The mere fact, however, that manufacturers and consumers are responding rationally to current incentives does not mean that all is well. On the contrary, the problems identified by environmentalists are real, and they will persist in the face of moral invective aimed at manufacturers and SUV drivers.

Indeed, these problems exist precisely because people are responding rationally to existing incentives.

The reason is that a family's safety on the road depends more on a vehicle's relative size than on its absolute size. If all families bought smaller vehicles, we would have a cleaner environment and no family's safety would be jeopardized.

But a family can only choose the size of its own vehicle. It cannot dictate what others buy. Any family that unilaterally bought a smaller vehicle might thus put itself at risk by unilaterally disarming.

Continued finger wagging by social critics will do nothing to stem the harm caused by sales growth of sport utility vehicles. Yet as a freedom-loving citizenry, few of us would want to empower bureaucrats to outlaw any vehicle they considered unfriendly to the environment.

The only practical remedy, given the undeniable fact that driving bulky, polluting vehicles causes damage to others, is to give ourselves an incentive to take this damage into account when deciding what vehicles to buy.

No one complains of intrusive government regulation when we tax trucks according to weight, because a truck's weight is a good indicator of how much damage it does to our roads.

Pegging passenger vehicle taxes to weight, emission levels, and fuel economy can be recommended on similar practical grounds.

If William Clay Ford feels uneasy about Ford's role in our current environmental problems, he and his fellow executives should abandon their historical opposition to such policies.

New York Times, May 16, 2000

8

Energy and the Environment

When gasoline is refined, toxic waste gases inflict heavy costs on people other than those who produce or consume the gasoline. Similarly, when people burn gasoline in their cars, they generate additional congestion and greenhouse gases that burden others. Economists call such spillover effects "negative externalities," and it is because of them that the invisible hand functions so poorly in energy markets.

When the production or consumption of a good generates negative externalities, the tendency is for too much of it to be produced and consumed. To curb the resulting damage, governments once favored a command-and-control approach in which regulations mandated or prohibited specific actions. For example, producers might be required to install filters on their smokestacks or limit their discharge of pollutants to some fraction of the amount emitted during a prior year. Motorists might be permitted to buy gasoline only on odd or even dates, according to the last digit on their license plate numbers, and so on.

The problem with this approach is that it takes no account of the fact that some people are more efficient than others at mitigating the effects of negative externalities. If our goal is, say, to reduce total emissions of sulfur dioxide by half, we want to achieve that goal at the lowest possible cost. But that's not what will happen if we require each and every producer to reduce SO_2 emissions by half.

To see why, suppose there are two firms that discharge SO_2 into the air in a given location and that each emits two hundred tons per day. One producer has an available technology that can reduce its emissions at a cost of $15 per ton, while the best technology available to the second producer costs $50 per ton. If we require each producer to reduce its emissions by half, the total cost will be $6,500 per day ($1,500 for the first producer plus $5,000 for the second). But suppose instead that we achieve our target by having the first firm eliminate its emissions entirely. The total cost would then be only $3,000 per day (all borne by the first firm), or less than half as much as when each producer cut emissions by 50 percent.

Anyone who doubts that the targeted approach is better need only remember that when the pie is bigger, everyone can have a bigger slice than before. If the alternative were to have both firms cut emissions by one hundred pounds per day, the second firm would be willing to pay the first firm at least $1,500 per day (the minimum amount required to make the first firm as well-off as under the original arrangement) and no more than $5,000 per day (the second firm's cost under the original arrangement).

The most efficient way of reducing pollution is virtually impossible to achieve by command-and-control regulation because regulators have no way of knowing the details of pollution abatement technologies available to different firms. Yet it is still possible to concentrate pollution reduction in the hands of those who can accomplish it at the lowest cost. One way is to levy a tax for each ton of pollution a firm emits. In response, firms that have access to technologies that can filter out pollution for less than the cost of the tax will have an incentive to adopt those technologies. Firms that do not have access to such technologies will find it cheaper to continue polluting and pay the tax.

The end result is a distribution of pollution abatement across firms that is both efficient and fair—efficient because firms that can reduce pollution most cheaply are the ones that reduce it, and fair because firms that do not have access to pollution abatement methods end up paying additional taxes.

THE columns included in this chapter consider specific examples of how tax policy can help us achieve a cleaner and less congested environment. In the first selection, which focuses on gasoline taxes, I argue that the intense political resistance to using taxes for this purpose is based on a fundamental misunderstanding of the underlying economic principles.

34. Why Are Sensible Policies Often "Politically Unthinkable"?

Suppose a politician promised to reveal the details of a simple proposal that could save hundreds of billions of dollars for American consumers, reduce traffic congestion, improve urban air quality, cut greenhouse gas emissions, and reduce dependence on Middle Eastern oil. The plan would require no net cash outlays from American families, no additional regulations, and no expansion of the bureaucracy.

As economists often remind their students, if something sounds too good to be true, it probably is. So this announcement would almost surely be greeted skeptically. Yet a policy that would deliver precisely the outcomes described could be enacted by Congress tomorrow—a $2-a-gallon tax on gasoline whose proceeds are refunded to American families in reduced payroll taxes.

Proposals of this sort have been advanced frequently in recent years by both liberal and conservative economists. Invariably, however, pundits dismiss these proposals as "politically unthinkable."

But if higher gasoline taxes would make everyone better off, why are they unthinkable? Part of the answer is suggested by the fate of the first serious proposal to employ gasoline taxes to reduce America's dependence on Middle Eastern oil. The year was 1979 and the country was still reeling from the second of two oil embargoes. To encourage conservation, President Jimmy Carter proposed a steep tax on gasoline, with the proceeds to be refunded in the form of lower payroll taxes.

Carter's opponents mounted a rhetorically brilliant attack on his proposal, arguing that because consumers would get back every cent they paid in gasoline taxes, they could, and would, buy just as much gasoline as before. Many found this argument compelling, and in the end, President Carter's proposal won just thirty-five votes in the House of Representatives.

The experience appears to have left an indelible imprint on political decision makers. To this day, many seem persuaded that tax-cum-rebate proposals do not make economic sense. But it is the argument advanced by Carter's critics that makes no sense. It betrays a fundamental misunderstanding of how such a program would alter people's opportunities and incentives.

Some examples help to illustrate how the program would work. On average, a family of four currently consumes almost two thousand gallons of gasoline annually. If all families continued to consume gasoline at the same rate after the imposition of a $2-a-gallon gasoline tax, the average family would pay $4,000 in additional gasoline taxes annually. A representative family with two earners would then receive an annual payroll tax refund of $4,000. So, if all other families continued to buy as much gasoline as before, then this family's tax rebate would enable it to do so as well, just as Carter's critics claimed.

But that is not how things would play out. Suppose, for example, that the family was about to replace its aging Ford Explorer, which gets fifteen miles per gallon. It could buy another Explorer. Or it could buy Ford's new Focus wagon, which has almost as much cargo capacity and gets more than thirty miles per gallon. The latter choice would save a whopping $2,000 annually at the pump. Not all families would switch, of course, but many would.

From the experience of the 1970s, we know that consumers respond to higher gasoline prices not just by buying more efficient cars, but also by taking fewer trips, forming carpools, and moving closer to work. If families overall bought half as much gasoline as before, the rebate would not be $2,000 per earner, but only $1,000. In that case, our representative two-earner family could not buy just as much gasoline as before unless it spent $2,000 less on everything else. So, contrary to Carter's critics, the tax-cum-rebate program would profoundly alter not only our incentives but also our opportunities.

A second barrier to the adoption of higher gasoline taxes is the belief held by proponents of smaller government that all taxes are bad. Vice President Dick Cheney, for example, has opposed higher gasoline taxes as inconsistent with the administration's belief that prices should be set by market forces. But as even the most enthusiastic free market economists concede, current gasoline prices are so low that they fail to reflect the environmental and foreign policy costs associated with gasoline consumption. Government would actually be smaller, and we would all be more prosperous, if not for the problems caused by what President Bush has called our addiction to oil.

At today's price of about $2.50 a gallon, a $2-a-gallon tax would raise prices by about 80 percent (leaving them still more than $1 a gallon below price levels in Europe). Evidence suggests that an increase of that magnitude would reduce consumption by more than 15 percent in the short run and almost 60 percent in the long run. These savings would be just the beginning, because higher prices would also intensify the race to bring new fuel efficient technologies to market.

The gasoline tax-cum-rebate proposal enjoys extremely broad support. Liberals favor it. Environmentalists favor it. The conservative Nobel laureate Gary S. Becker has endorsed it, as has the antitax crusader Grover Norquist. President Bush's former chief economist, N. Gregory Mankiw, has advanced it repeatedly.

In the warmer weather they will have inherited from us a century from now, perspiring historians will struggle to explain why this proposal was once considered politically unthinkable.

New York Times, February 16, 2006

PEOPLE have *very* strong opinions about tax policy. By a wide margin, the preceding column generated a larger volume of reader responses than any other in this collection. A large proportion of my correspondents conceded that making gasoline more expensive might have some desirable consequences but felt that my proposed tax increase would be harmful on balance to them. The next selection is my response to many of the specific concerns raised by these readers.

35. Why Do Gasoline Taxes Put More Money in People's Pockets?

Historians argue about whether the admonition "First, do no harm" actually appeared in the original Hippocratic oath. But no one disputes that it is sound advice, not just for physicians but also for others entrusted to act on our behalf. Yet many government officials seem to ignore it. For example, the recent spike in gasoline prices has prompted a wave of proposals that if enacted would do far more harm than good.

Senator John Thune, Republican of South Dakota, among others, has advocated suspension of the federal gasoline tax of 18.4 cents a gallon. Similar proposals to suspend state taxes have been advanced in New York and at least twelve other states. These proposals make no economic sense. Tax suspensions promise only illusory relief in the short run and would actually create new financial burdens for consumers in the long run.

An immediate problem is that a tax cut would be offset in part by OPEC's response to it. The Organization of the Petroleum Exporting Countries sets its price target with an eye toward what motorists are able to pay. Dealing with OPEC is thus like dealing with a rational kidnapper, whose demands are governed by the ability of the victim's family to pay. A visible transfer of money to the victim's family (like an inheritance) would only increase the kidnapper's ransom demand. Similarly, since OPEC now realizes that motorists are able to pay $3 a gallon, its best response to a gasoline tax cut would be to raise the price of oil by enough to keep gasoline prices at $3.

A more general problem is that reducing gasoline taxes would promote inefficient consumption patterns. The lost revenues would also require some combination of increasing other taxes, borrowing more money from abroad (which taxpayers would have to repay in full, with interest), and enacting further cuts in valued public services.

Gasoline prices are rising because the world's appetite for oil has been outstripping dwindling supplies. Legislatures cannot repeal the law of supply and demand. To escape the burden of widespread energy shortages, we must consume less energy. And to achieve that goal, gasoline prices need to be higher, not lower.

The most efficient means to that end is thus precisely the opposite of what Senator Thune proposes. In my February 16 column, I suggested an additional gasoline tax of $2 a gallon. All revenue would go into a common pool, which would then be returned on an approximately equal per capita basis by reducing payroll taxes.

Because rebates for individual consumers would be independent of the amount of gasoline tax they paid, the higher post-tax gasoline prices would strongly encourage conservation. This would reduce our dependence on foreign oil, as well as alleviate congestion and pollution. And just as cutting the gasoline tax cut would encourage future OPEC price increases, increasing it would discourage them.

As with all such proposals, the devil is in the details. Because the losers from any policy change cry more loudly than the winners sing, a tax increase would be palatable only if the resulting economic gains were distributed equitably.

Readers were quick to identify deficiencies in my proposed payroll tax rebate. It would not help retirees, for example, because they no longer pay this tax. The rebate for retirees could instead take the form of an augmented Social Security payment. (Because retirees typically drive less than workers, this supplement should be smaller than the payroll tax rebate.)

Businesses could also receive rebates, which could be based on historical patterns of fuel consumption by industry and company size. To promote efficiency, the critical design feature is that the rebate for each business be independent of its current gasoline consumption.

Would a steep gasoline tax jeopardize automakers like Ford and General Motors, whose current product lines emphasize light trucks and sport utility vehicles? It would shift demand away from such vehicles to more fuel-efficient ones, but automakers could respond by altering their product mix. The transition could be smoothed by announcing a start date well in the future—say, January 1, 2010—and then phasing in the tax gradually, say, by ten-cent monthly increments.

What about motorists who could not afford to buy new fuel-efficient cars? A gradual phase-in would also provide valuable transition time for these drivers. They could retire their current vehicles within a few years in favor of more recent used models with better fuel economy. Rebates could also be made progressive.

Another reader's concern was that the new tax might be inflationary. But unlike the gasoline price increases of the 1970s, which sent hundreds of billions of dollars to OPEC, tax revenues would remain in the United States. The prices of products whose production or delivery is intensive in gasoline use would rise because of the tax. But even now, the gasoline required to produce these products imposes environmental and foreign policy costs on Americans. To the extent that higher gasoline prices encouraged conservation, they would be offset by lower costs elsewhere.

An academic economist clearly runs less risk than a politician in proposing higher gasoline taxes. But how much political risk would such a proposal really entail? According to a recent *New York Times/CBS News* poll, 55 percent of Americans would be willing to support a higher gasoline tax if it reduced dependence on foreign oil. Given that widely reported finding, proposing to suspend gasoline taxes in the midst of pervasive energy shortages will strike no one as bold political leadership. It might strike some as an unconscionable pander.

It may be naive to expect our current crop of leaders to take affirmative steps to alleviate the energy crisis. But elections are coming. And in the meantime, surely we can demand that politicians do no further harm.

New York Times, June 8, 2006

WHAT motivates many policy makers to try to peg prices below marginal cost is a desire to avoid imposing undue hardships on low-income persons. But because artificially low prices invariably encourage wasteful use patterns, they make the economic pie smaller than it would have been if prices had been equal to marginal cost.

In the following selection, written during the 2008 presidential primaries, I try to explain why neither John McCain nor Hillary Clinton found economists willing to endorse their proposed summer holiday from the federal gasoline tax.

36. Are Inefficient Policies Ever a Good Way to Help the Poor?

Adam Smith's modern disciples are more enthusiastic about his celebrated invisible hand idea than he ever was. In their account, Smith asserted that purely selfish individuals are led by an invisible hand to produce the greatest good for all. Yet Smith himself was under no such illusion.

On the contrary, the relevant quotation from his *Wealth of Nations,* which describes a profit-seeking business owner, is far more circumspect. It says that this owner "is in this, as in many other cases, led by an invisible hand to promote an end which was no part of his intention." It continues, "Nor is it always the worse for the society that it was no part of it. By pursuing his own interest he frequently promotes that of the society more effectually than when he really intends to promote it."

In short, Smith understood that the invisible hand is often benign, but not always.

This understanding has important implications for economic policy in general, and for the recent presidential campaign dust-up about gasoline taxes in particular.

If you believe, with Smith's modern disciples, that unfettered pursuit of self-interest always promotes society's interests, you probably view all taxes as a regrettable evil, necessary to pay for roads and national security, but also an unwelcome drag on economic efficiency. The problem, according to this view, is that taxes distort the price signals through which the invisible hand guides resources to their best destinations.

Smith's more nuanced position supports a different view of taxes. When market prices convey accurate signals of cost and value, the invisible hand promotes the common good. But prices often diverge from cost and value and, in those cases, taxes can actually help steer resources toward more highly valued uses.

It's helpful to look more closely at why the invisible hand works so well in many ordinary markets. In the market for potatoes, for example, production and consumption are determined by millions of separate cost-benefit calculations. Profit-seeking sellers are willing to offer an additional pound of potatoes for sale whenever the benefit of doing so—as measured by what buyers are willing to pay—is enough to cover the cost of production.

The market reaches equilibrium when the cost of producing the last pound is exactly equal to its value. If the costs incurred directly by sellers are the only relevant costs of expanding potato production, and if the benefits to potato buyers are the only relevant benefits, the invisible hand gets things just right.

The production and consumption of many other goods, however, generate costs or benefits that fall on people besides buyers and sellers. Producing an extra gallon of gasoline, for example, generates not just additional costs to producers, but also pollution costs that fall on others. As before, market forces cause production to expand until the seller's direct cost for the last unit sold is exactly the value of that unit to the buyer. But because each gallon of gasoline also generates external pollution costs, the total cost of that last gallon produced is higher than its value to consumers.

The upshot is that gasoline consumption is inefficiently high. Suppose that pollution costs are $2 for the last gallon consumed, but that its $4 price at the pump is just enough to cover its direct production costs. Reducing production and consumption by a gallon would then cause consumers to lose fuel that they value at $4, which would be exactly offset by the $4 in reduced production costs. The $2 in reduced pollution costs would thus be a net gain for society.

That simple example captures the classic breakdown in the invisible hand when a product's market price doesn't reflect all its relevant social costs and benefits. In such cases, the simplest solution is to discourage consumption by taxing it.

Doing so would not just raise revenue to pay for public services; it would also allocate society's resources more efficiently. This explains economists' almost universal dismay when Senators John McCain and Hillary Rodham Clinton recently proposed eliminating the federal tax on gasoline for the summer.

The stated aim of their proposal was to ease the financial burden of sharply higher gasoline prices. But adopting inefficient policies is never the best way to help people in financial distress.

Efficiency is important because any policy that enlarges the economic pie necessarily lets everyone have a bigger slice than before. Economists opposed suspending the gas tax because doing so would make the economic pie smaller.

Of course, when millions of voters feel the pinch of rapidly rising prices, politicians find it hard to stand idly by. But as the late economist Abba Lerner once remarked, the main problem confronting the poor is that they have too little money. The best solution is not to reduce the prices they pay but rather to bolster their income, for example, by selectively reducing the payroll tax for low-income workers or increasing the earned income tax credit.

Suspending the gas tax would encourage rich and poor alike to do more summer driving. It would also promote sales of fuel intensive vehicles. Because the gas tax reduces waste, it actually makes more resources available to help low-income families.

Gasoline is one of a host of goods whose production or consumption generates costs that fall on outsiders. Noisy goods, like leaf blowers, for example, can jolt whole neighborhoods from calm. And goods that don't biodegrade readily, like many plastic bags, can generate costly waste streams. The list goes on.

That the invisible hand often breaks down is actually good news. After all, we need to tax something to pay for public services. By taxing forms of consumption that generate negative side effects, we could generate enough revenue to eliminate budget deficits, as well as help steer resources toward their most highly valued uses.

Because such taxes make the economy more efficient, it makes no sense to object that they impose hardships on low-income families. Again, an efficient policy is one that maximizes the size of the economic pie. And with a bigger pie, everyone can get a bigger slice.

New York Times, May 25, 2008

DESIGNING and implementing sensible economic policies within the borders of a single country is difficult enough. In the next selection, I explain why even the most successful attempts can sometimes be compromised when bad economic policies are adopted in other countries.

37. How Do Fuel Subsidies Abroad Make Americans Poorer?

When countries adopted bad economic policies in decades past, their own citizens paid the price. In today's globalized economy, however, the burden falls more broadly.

A case in point is the use of fuel subsidies to protect citizens of developing economies from rising prices. As Keith Bradsher recently reported in the *New York Times*, many emerging economies employ subsidies that keep domestic fuel prices far below the world price. As a result, these countries consume far more fuel than they would otherwise.

By one estimate, countries with fuel subsidies accounted for virtually the entire increase in worldwide oil consumption last year. Without this artificial demand stimulus, world oil prices would have been significantly lower. Earlier this summer, for example, world oil prices fell by $4 a barrel on news that reduced subsidies would increase Chinese domestic fuel prices by about 17 percent.

It is unrealistic to expect other governments to abandon subsidies just so Americans who drive SUVs and live in big houses can benefit from lower world energy prices. But those governments might want to reconsider their policy in the light of overwhelming economic evidence that the subsidies create net losses even for their ostensible beneficiaries.

To be sure, higher fuel prices produce economic suffering. The unfortunate reality, however, is that when the price of an imported resource rises in the world market, buyers must take a hit. Subsidizing fuel does nothing to reduce the inevitable suffering, and actually makes it worse.

The problem is that when a good is priced below its cost, people use it wastefully. In the case of a gallon of gasoline, the cost to a country is the value of every additional sacrifice that its use entails. That includes not just the price of buying the gallon in the world market— say, $4—but also external costs, like dirtier air and increased congestion. The external costs are often hard to measure but are nonetheless substantial. With reasonable estimates factored in for them, the true cost of using a gallon is clearly greater than $4. By contrast, the price of gasoline to users is simply the amount they pay at the pump. With a $2-a-gallon subsidy in effect, gasoline bought in the world market at $4 would sell for $2, or more than $2 less than its true economic cost.

Consider how this difference might affect a trucker's decision about whether to accept a hauling job. A rational trucker will apply the basic cost-benefit test, which says that something is worth doing if, and only if, its benefit is at least as great as its cost. Suppose the job in question requires 1,000 gallons of fuel, available at the subsidized price of $2 a gallon, for a total fuel outlay of $2,000. If the cost of the trucker's time and equipment are, say, $1,000 for the trip, his narrow interests dictate accepting the job if the shipper is willing to pay at least $3,000. Suppose the shipper is willing to pay that amount but not more.

The problem is that if the trucker accepts the job at that price, the country as a whole will be worse off by more than $2,000. Although the $3,000 fee would cover his own costs, the government would end up paying $2,000 in additional subsidies for the 1,000 gallons consumed. On top of that, the trip would generate additional pollution and congestion costs. So the fact that the subsidy encouraged him to accept the job means that its net effect is equivalent to throwing more than $2,000 onto a bonfire.

Waste is always bad. Anyone who doubts it need only remember that when the economic pie grows, it is always possible for everyone to have a larger slice than before. Using fuel for activities whose costs exceed their benefits makes the economic pie smaller.

Subsidy proponents cite the firestorm of political protest that would erupt if fuel were to sell at the international market price. That fuel subsidies are wasteful, however, implies that there must be less costly ways to keep the peace.

Consider again our trucker who accepted a job that barely covered the cost of his time, equipment, and subsidized fuel. Instead of paying $2,000 to subsidize his fuel, the government could give him a tax cut of, say, $1,000, and use the remaining $1,000 to help pay for public services. Because the trucker earned only enough from the hauling job to cover his costs at the subsidized fuel price, he would be $1,000 better off with the tax cut alone than with the fuel subsidy. The additional support for public services would augment this benefit. In short, a tax cut is always a better way to keep political protest at bay because, unlike a fuel subsidy, it does not encourage shipments whose costs exceed their benefits.

If a U.S. president urged developing economies to eliminate fuel subsidies because they result in higher energy prices for Americans, the conversation would probably end very quickly. But let's reframe this conversation.

We could start by heeding the same advice we'd like others to follow. Emerging economies are not the only ones in which prices at the pump substantially understate the true social cost of fuel. For instance, although the United States doesn't have direct fuel subsidies, existing fuel taxes significantly understate the pollution and congestion costs associated with additional fuel use. Adopting some variant of a tax on carbon, as both leading presidential candidates have proposed, would help eliminate this discrepancy.

That would set the stage for our next president to explain to other leaders why eliminating fuel subsidies would make the overall economic pie larger. Because the resulting efficiency gains can be redistributed so that everyone gets a bigger slice than before, the idea should be fairly easy to sell.

New York Times, August 16, 2008

CRITICS often accuse economists of failing to appreciate the extent to which human behavior is shaped by cultural forces. But many people also fail to appreciate the extent to which cultural norms and practices are themselves shaped by economic forces. In the last selection in this chapter, I examine the American public's fleeting love affair with the sport utility vehicle.

38. What Happens If the Herd Changes Course?

The herd instinct is as powerful in humans as in other animal species.

Anyone who doubts it should rent *What Do You Say to a Naked Lady?*, the 1970 film by Allen Funt, the creator of *Candid Camera.* The money scene portrays a man responding to a help wanted ad. He is directed to a waiting room occupied by men who appear to be other job seekers but are actually Funt's confederates. At no apparent signal, these men stand and begin to disrobe. The hapless job seeker's dismay is evident, but after a few moments, he too stands and disrobes. At scene's end, the men are standing naked, apparently waiting for whatever comes next.

Clearly the herd instinct can lead us astray. For the most part, however, the impulse to emulate others serves us well. After all, without drawing on the wisdom and experience of others, it would be almost impossible to cope with the stream of complex decisions we confront.

Economists increasingly recognize the importance of herd behavior in explaining ordinary purchase decisions. A case in point is the sport utility vehicle. Herd behavior helps us understand not only the explosive rise of this market segment in the 1990s but also its imminent collapse.

The Chevrolet Suburban (or, as Dave Barry called it, the Chevrolet Subdivision) has been produced since 1935, but it and similar vehicles were originally used almost exclusively for commercial purposes. Before the appearance of the Jeep Wagoneer in 1963 and the Ford Bronco in 1966, the family SUV segment essentially did not exist. As recently as 1975, it accounted for only 2 percent of total vehicle sales.

In the 1990s, however, it became perhaps the biggest success story in automotive history. From a base of only 750,000 units in 1990, annual SUV sales reached almost 3 million by 2000. In 2003, 23 percent of vehicles sold in the United States were SUVs.

The conventional determinants of consumer demand cannot explain this astonishing trajectory. Cheap fuel was a contributing factor, but fuel had also been cheap in earlier decades. Similarly, rising average income could not have been decisive, because the pre-SUV decades had experienced even more rapid income growth.

Why wealthier people would want to switch from cars to truck-based SUVs is not obvious. Many engineers who helped design these vehicles expressed wonder that they have sold in such numbers. Early ads, coupled with names like Blazer and Pathfinder, stressed the vehicles' off-road capabilities. But as one engineer quipped, the only time most SUVs actually go off the road is when inebriated owners miss their driveways.

Nor can safety concerns explain the success of SUVs. As Keith Bradsher, a reporter for the *New York Times,* explains in his 2002 book, *High and Mighty,* their weight confers some advantage in head-on collisions with smaller vehicles (at the expense of occupants of those vehicles), but their poor handling, high propensity to roll over, and longer stopping distances make them more dangerous, on balance, than cars.

Nor, finally, is the greater cargo capacity of SUVs enough to explain their popularity, as minivans and station wagons offer similar capacity without the handling and mileage penalties.

To understand the explosive growth of SUV sales, we must look first to changes in demand caused by new patterns of income growth and then to how others responded to those changes. Unlike the first three postwar decades, when income grew at about the same rate for people at all income levels, the period since the mid-1970s has seen most income growth accrue to the wealthy. That change helped persuade Land Rover, then a British-owned company, to bring its premium Range Rover to the United States in 1987, at the then astonishingly high base price of $31,375.

Although Range Rover initially had the luxury SUV market to itself, and top earners could easily afford one, early sales were modest. A turning point was its appearance in the 1992 Robert Altman film, *The Player.* The film's lead character, the studio executive Griffin Mill (played by Tim Robbins), could have bought any vehicle he pleased. His choice? A Range Rover with a fax machine in the dashboard.

An important feature of the herd instinct is that people are more likely to emulate those with higher incomes. Seeing a wealthy studio executive behind the wheel of a Range Rover instantly certified it as a player's ride. As more and more high-income buyers purchased these vehicles, their allure grew. And when other automakers began offering similar vehicles at lower prices, SUV sales took off.

But what the herd instinct giveth, it also taketh away. Even when gasoline was still relatively inexpensive, many urban motorists had begun to question the merits of owning poor-handling off-road vehicles that got only ten miles a gallon. And with gas now selling for more than $3 a gallon, the cachet of SUVs has vanished completely. If driving one was once like having a T-shirt saying, "I'm a player," it is now more like having one saying, "I'm a chump."

And that is a perception that no product can long survive. With unsold inventory languishing on dealer lots, prices of SUVs have been plummeting. In some markets, GM is offering subsidized gas at $1.99 a gallon (and Ford is offering $1,000 worth of free gas) to potential buyers.

The last of Ford's mammoth Excursions rolled off its Louisville, Kentucky, assembly line last September 30. And GM's largest SUV, the Hummer H1, was discontinued in June of this year.

With the herd now in full stampede, the era of big, gas-guzzling SUVs may soon be history.

New York Times, August 3, 2006

9

Winner-Take-All Markets

John Maynard Keynes once compared investing in the stock market to picking the winner of a beauty contest. In each case, it's not who you think will win, but who you think others will pick. The same characterization increasingly applies to a student's choice among universities. This choice depends much less now on what any individual student may think, and much more on what panels of experts think. The *U.S. News & World Report*'s annual college ranking issue has become the magazine's biggest seller by far, and the same is true of *Business Week*'s biennial issue ranking the nation's top MBA programs. The size of a school's applicant pool fluctuates sharply in response to even minor movements in these rankings.

Hierarchy in education is nothing new, of course, and it has always been important. But as every ambitious college applicant is keenly aware, it has become far more important than in the past. Why this change? The short answer is that the economic reward for elite educational credentials has jumped sharply in recent decades.

Behind this jump lies the spread and intensification of what economist Philip Cook and I have called winner-take-all markets, in which small differences in performance (or even small differences in the credentials used to predict performance) translate into extremely large differences in reward.

Such markets have long been familiar in entertainment and sports. The best soprano may be only marginally better than the second best, but in a world in which most people listen to music on compact discs, there is little need for the second best. In such a world, the best soprano may earn a seven-figure annual salary while the second best struggles to get by. In similar fashion, new technologies allow us to clone the services of the most talented performers in a growing number of occupations, thereby enabling them to serve ever broader and more lucrative markets.

The market for tax advice, for example, was once served by a large army of local practitioners, but is increasingly dominated by the developers of a small handful of software programs. Scores of programs competed for reviewer approval in the early stages of this transition. But once opinion leaders anointed Intuit's TurboTax and Kiplinger's TaxCut as the most comprehensive, user-friendly programs, competing programs faced a nearly impossible task.

A constellation of factors helps us understand why similar shakeouts have occurred in industry after industry. The information revolution has made us more aware of product quality differences and puts us in direct contact with the world's best suppliers. Sharply reduced transportation costs and tariff barriers enable these suppliers to ship their products to us more cheaply than before. Research and development costs and other fixed costs now comprise a larger share of total costs, making it harder for small producers to achieve efficient scale.

Also contributing to the winner-take-all trend is the increasing concern among affluent buyers with product rank per se. For example, whereas the demand for any given make of car was once based largely on functional characteristics like size, reliability, and fuel economy, buyers increasingly search for something more. They want a fast car, one that handles well, or one that stands out from the crowd. These characteristics are far more context-dependent than fuel economy and reliability. How fast does a car have to be to impress the potential buyer? If a car produced in 1925 could reach 60 miles per hour *eventually*, the driver would have experienced it as breathtakingly exciting, a *really* fast car. Today if your car does not get from 0 to 60 miles per hour in under six seconds, it doesn't *seem* like a fast car. Context-sensitive characteristics like speed and handling dictate an increasing share of purchase decisions in automobile markets. And when what people want is defined in relative terms, only a limited number of suppliers can deliver. In the extreme case, only a single company can truthfully claim to offer the fastest car in the market.

One result of the movement toward winner-take-all markets is the exploding salaries paid to the handful of key players most responsible for an organization's success. CEOs of the largest American corporations, for example, have seen their incomes rise more than tenfold since the late 1970s, a period during which the post-tax income of the top 1 percent of U.S. earners more than tripled.

THE selected columns in this chapter explore the causes and consequences of winner-take-all markets. In the first one, I discuss the role of technologies that allow the most able performers to extend their reach.

39. How Do Cloning Technologies Create Winner-Take-All Markets?

In the early 1980s, a friend's wife paid a voice impersonator to tape the greeting for her husband's answering machine as a gift. "Well, John's just not home at the moment," the tape began, in a voice eerily like former President Ronald Reagan's. "But if you'll leave your name and number, Nancy or I will have him get back to you as soon as possible." In the summer of 2001, AT&T announced a breakthrough in synthesized speech software that will put many voice impersonators out of business.

The new approach uses fragments of sounds culled from recordings of a subject's voice to recreate speech from printed text. In time, this software will render a lifelike facsimile of someone's voice saying things that he or she never actually said. Archival recordings will even make it possible to reproduce the voices of people long dead.

Assuming that AT&T perfects its process and that people retain rights to their own voices, who will be the ultimate winners and losers?

Voice cloning is just one of many technologies that expand the market reach of the economy's most able performers. These technologies increase our national wealth, but they also cause it to be distributed far more unequally. The invention of movies, for example, enabled a small cadre of highly talented stars to displace thousands of less talented stage actors in local theaters.

The new synthetic voices will replace the voices currently used in applications like car navigation systems and message systems, and clones of celebrity voices will be used in radio and television commercials.

The voices of noncelebrities will not command high prices, since there is a large number of people who could supply the voice templates for them. Still, the technology will make it possible to use only the best voices for these purposes. People with less perfect voices who are now in this line of work will be displaced. This is a net gain, since we will get announcements of higher quality and the displaced people will be freed up for other useful tasks. But most of them will probably earn less, since for most of them a recording job was their best option.

The changes from celebrity voice cloning promise to be more sweeping. Increasingly, advertisers are using the voices of celebrities in national radio and television commercials. So far, however, the expense of taping messages specifically tailored to each location has mostly excluded these voices from local commercials. Voice cloning will change that. The voices announcing this week's sales at neighborhood supermarkets, for example, could soon be those of, say, Tom Hanks or Whoopi Goldberg.

Some celebrities command more viewer attention than others. That explains why sponsors pay someone like Michael Jordan as much as $40 million a year while most celebrities are of little or no value in the endorsement market. No one yet knows whose voices will prove most effective. But once the winners are identified, intensive bidding to acquire rights to their voice templates will begin.

In short, voice cloning, like other similar technologies, will create a winner-take-all market in which small differences in performance give rise to large differences in economic reward. Technologies like this one have been rapidly transforming the American economic landscape. Authors of the best tax advice software have displaced thousands of local tax accountants, and the best Internet auction site has displaced thousands of local retailers. In countless arenas this phenomenon of duplication and distribution enables the best performers to serve ever broader markets.

Since cloning frees up resources while giving us services of higher quality, society benefits. But the downside is that the monetary value of these gains is distributed unequally. The spread of winner-take-all markets helps explain why almost all recent gains in income and wealth have gone to a relatively small number of people atop the economic pyramid.

In the 2000 presidential campaign, Al Gore was unable to persuade a sufficiently large majority of American voters that tax cuts for top earners make little sense in such an economy. But once AT&T clones Franklin Delano Roosevelt's eloquent baritone, Democratic strategists will have a new weapon. In our era of sharply rising inequality, would Bush's razor-thin margin have withstood an updated series of FDR's fireside chats questioning the wisdom of massive tax cuts for the wealthy?

New York Times, August 7, 2001

AMONG many economists, it has always been an article of faith that market forces steer people to the jobs that make the best use of their talents. But economists also recognize circumstances under which that faith is unjustified. Consider, for example, a person who must decide between continuing to earn his living as an independent fisherman or working for $500 a week in a factory. Let's suppose this person considers the two equivalent except for the matter of salary, and that he would earn $501 a week if he continued fishing. Economists would then predict that he would continue fishing but would add that his decision might not be best for society as a whole. If he continues fishing, some of the fish he would catch would otherwise have been caught by other fishermen. So if we take into account the negative effect of his presence on the income of other fishermen, society's total income is likely to be smaller if he continues fishing than if he worked in the factory.

In the next selection, written at the height of the financial boom in 2007, I suggest that incentives created by winner-take-all markets often lead to similar misallocations.

40. Do We Have Too Many Hedge Fund Managers?

What are the career aspirations of the nation's most accomplished and ambitious students these days? I haven't seen a formal survey, but a rapidly growing percentage of the best students I teach say they want to manage hedge funds or private equity firms.

Little wonder. According to Institutional Investor's *Alpha* magazine, the hedge fund manager James Simons earned $1.7 billion last year, and two other managers earned more than $1 billion. The combined income of the top twenty-five hedge fund managers exceeded $14 billion in 2006.

These managers also enjoy remarkably favorable tax treatment. For example, even though "carried interest" (mainly their 20 percent commission on portfolio gains) has the look and feel of ordinary income, it is taxed at the 15 percent capital gains rate rather than the 35 percent top rate for ordinary income. That provision alone saved Simons several hundred million dollars in taxes last year.

Congress is now considering a proposal to tax carried interest as ordinary income. To no one's surprise, private equity lobbyists were quick to insist that doing so would cause grave economic damage. The deals brokered by their clients often create enormous value, to be sure. Yet the proposed legislation would not block a single transaction worth doing. What is more, economic analysis suggests that it would actually increase production in other sectors of the economy by reducing wasteful overcrowding in the market for aspiring portfolio managers.

This market is what economists call a winner-take-all market, essentially a tournament in which a handful of winners are selected from a much larger field of initial contestants. Such markets tend to attract too many contestants for two reasons.

The first is an information bias. An intelligent decision about whether to enter any tournament requires an accurate estimate of the odds of winning. Yet people's assessments of their relative skill levels are notoriously optimistic. Surveys show, for example, that more than 90 percent of workers consider themselves more productive than their average colleague.

This overconfidence bias is likely to distort career choice because, in addition to the motivational forces that support it, the biggest winners in many tournaments are so conspicuous. For example, NBA stars who earn eight-figure salaries appear on television several nights a week, whereas the thousands who failed to make the league attract little notice.

Similarly, hedge fund managers with ten-figure incomes are far more visible than the legions of contestants who never made the final cut. When people overestimate their chances of winning, too many forsake productive occupations in traditional markets to compete in winner-take-all markets.

A second reason for persistent overcrowding in winner-take-all markets is a structural problem known as tragedy of the commons.

This problem helps explain, for instance, why we see too many gold prospectors, an occupation that has much in common with prospecting for corporate deals. In the initial stages of exploiting a newly discovered gold field, adding another prospector may significantly increase the total amount of gold found. Beyond some point, however, additional prospectors contribute little. The gold found by a newcomer to a crowded field is largely gold that would have been found by existing searchers.

A simple numerical example helps illustrate why private incentives often lead to wasteful overcrowding under these circumstances. Consider a man who must choose whether to work as an engineer for $100,000 or prospect for gold. Suppose he considers the nonfinancial aspects of the two careers equally attractive and expects to find $110,000 in gold if he becomes a prospector, $90,000 of which would have been found in his absence by existing prospectors. Self-interest would then dictate a career in prospecting, since $110,000 exceeds the $100,000 engineering salary. But because his efforts would increase the total value of gold found by only $20,000, society's total income would have been $80,000 higher had he become an engineer.

Similar incentives confront aspiring portfolio managers. Beyond some point, adding another highly paid manager produces little increase in industry commissions on managed investments. As in a crowded real estate market, the additional manager's commissions come largely at the expense of commissions that would have been generated by existing managers. So here too private incentives result in wasteful overcrowding.

Matthew Rhodes-Kropf, a finance professor at Columbia Business School, has argued that higher taxes on hedge fund and private equity firm managers are bad economic policy. "Private equity is a very important part of our economy," he said, adding that higher taxes will discourage it. Others have characterized the proposed legislation as envy-driven class warfare.

Both objections miss the essential point. No one denies that the talented people who guide capital to its most highly valued uses perform a vital service for society. But at any given moment, there are only so many deals to be struck. Sending ever larger numbers of our most talented graduates out to prospect for them has a high opportunity cost yet adds little economic value.

By making the after-tax rewards in the investment industry a little less spectacular, the proposed legislation would raise the attractiveness of other career paths, ones in which extra talent would yield substantial gains. And the additional tax revenue could pay for things that clearly need doing. For example, we could reduce the number of children who currently lack health insurance or reduce the number of cargo containers that enter our ports without being inspected.

Opponents of higher taxes often invoke the celebrated trade-off between equity and efficiency. But that objection makes no sense here. Ending preferential tax treatment of portfolio managers' earnings would serve both goals at once.

New York Times, July 5, 2007

MERGERS and acquisitions lawyers receive only a small percentage of the money involved in the transactions they oversee. But the amounts involved are often staggering—some $25 billion for the RJR-Nabisco buyout, for instance. When scores of lawyers split just one-quarter of 1 percent, we are still talking about a great deal of money for a few weeks or months of work.

These sums are on conspicuous display in the news media, causing many bright and ambitious young persons to ask themselves, "How can I get a job as a Wall Street lawyer?" With so many applicants vying for each entry-level opening, Wall Street firms can be extremely choosy. A degree from a top law school is required just to land an interview at some leading firms. And who ultimately gains admission to a top law school? The leading students from a handful of prestigious undergraduate institutions.

Our best and brightest high school seniors know that these institutions have increasingly become the gatekeepers for society's top-paying jobs. Years ago, many of these students attended state universities close to home, where they often received excellent educations at reasonable expense to their families. Today, these same students are far more likely to apply to, be accepted by, and to matriculate at one of a handful of the nation's most highly regarded universities.

Those universities, in turn, have redoubled their efforts to attract the most qualified applicants. In the following selection, I explain why this heightened competition is causing merit-based financial aid to displace traditional need-based aid.

41. Why Is Merit-Based Aid Crowding Out Need-Based Aid?

Consider the awkward decision confronting the admissions director of a highly selective university that is trying to move up in the academic pecking order (one of, say, 50 institutions whose administrators believe it would have landed in the top 10 this year except for various flaws in the rankings formulas).

On the director's desk sit the folders for two applicants. They have almost the same credentials, but one is just a little better than the other. She has a 4.2 grade point average, the other just a 4.0. She attained a combined score of 2370 on her SATs, the other only 2160. Her family has an annual income of $500,000, the other's only $30,000.

Now, as in the past, both students would be admitted. Years ago, the financial aid packages for these students would have been tailored in a way that would strike most people as just: the low-income student would have received a large aid package and the high-income student no aid at all. And both probably would have enrolled.

No longer. Now, the slightly better qualified student is likely to be lured elsewhere unless the director can match the substantial merit scholarships she has been offered by other institutions.

But coming up with extra money for her means having to offer a much smaller aid package to the slightly less qualified applicant, notwithstanding her family's economic need. In brief, universities' traditional commitment to need-based financial aid is under siege.

This change in large part is a result of the great economic reward of having a degree from an elite institution. The steep rise in overall earnings inequality over the past three decades has occurred in virtually every industry and occupation.

Even among entry-level jobs, a handful of elite positions now pay several times as much as the average job in each category. Competition for these jobs is fierce. For every starting analyst's position posted by J.P. Morgan, for example, the firm receives mail sacks full of applications. Employers in this situation seldom find time to interview applicants who did not graduate from an elite university.

Ambitious high school students have responded by applying in record numbers to the nation's most selective universities. But there is no greater number of slots in these institutions than before. And as the many thousands of highly qualified applicants who were rejected can attest, the admissions hurdle at top universities has become all but insurmountable. Some now reject ten or more applicants for each one they accept.

If so many highly qualified students are clamoring for admission to the best universities, why do these institutions feel such pressure to offer merit aid? The answer is that they need top students as much as top students need them. Indeed, several popular national rankings formulas are based in part on the average SAT score of a university's entering freshmen. So, to lay credible claim to elite status, a university must attract not only a renowned faculty but also the top-scoring freshmen each year.

To lure such students, other top students are often the most effective bait. Thus, according to one study, applicants typically seek an institution whose average combined SAT score is roughly one hundred points higher than their own. The ideal university, it seems, has much in common with Garrison Keillor's mythical Lake Wobegon, where "all the children are above average."

With median SAT scores in the nation's elite institutions rising steadily over time, bidding for superstar applicants has intensified accordingly. Top-scoring students are an asset whose value has been appreciating more rapidly than Manhattan real estate.

If success in attracting these students tends to be self-reinforcing, so does failure. Losing even a few of them to a rival university can set off a downward spiral, making a university less attractive to other top students as well as to distinguished faculty who prefer working with such students.

Institutions aspiring to elite status thus have little choice but to bid aggressively for top-scoring students. And hence the growing tendency for merit-based financial aid to displace need-based financial aid.

Many elite institutions were once party to an agreement in which they pledged to direct their limited financial aid money toward students with the greatest financial need. The Justice Department, animated by its belief that unbridled competition always and everywhere leads to the best outcome, took a dim view of this agreement. In 1991, it charged an alliance of twenty-three elite universities with violating the Sherman Antitrust Act by agreeing not to compete with merit-based financial aid packages for students admitted to more than one member institution.

In response, twenty-two institutions pledged to end their cooperation on financial aid decisions. (That the Massachusetts Institute of Technology refused to sign the pledge had little practical impact, since it could not continue to collude on aid packages without its former partners.)

The Justice Department was literally correct, of course, that the agreement was anticompetitive. Its explicit purpose was to preserve need-based financial aid by curbing competition for students with star credentials.

But why was that a bad thing? As economists since Adam Smith have persuasively argued, competition often generates enormous economic benefits, but not always. When reward depends strongly on rank, as in higher education, behavior that looks attractive to each institution often proves self-defeating from the perspective of society as a whole.

In such situations, collusive agreements can create gains for everyone. Of course, such agreements can also cause harm, as in the notorious price-fixing cases of antitrust lore. The challenge is to make informed distinctions.

Antitrust authorities may want to reconsider their belief that unlimited competition leads to the greatest good in every situation. Collective agreements should be scrutinized not on quasi-religious grounds but according to the practical test of whether they limit the harmful effects of competition without compromising its many benefits. The collective agreement among universities to protect need-based financial aid clearly met that test.

New York Times, April 14, 2005

EACH year more movies are produced and more books published than ever before. Yet each year a growing proportion of movie ticket and book sales are accounted for by a relatively small handful of the most popular entries in each category. In the next selection, written shortly after the publication of J. K. Rowling's fourth Harry Potter novel, I examine some of the forces that explain this pattern.

42. Will Children's Books Eventually Disappear?

Artist Gary Larson published a *Far Side* cartoon a few years ago under the heading "Optimistic Parents." A boy with a glazed expression sits clutching a joystick as he plays a video game, his parents watching from the doorway. A thought bubble above their heads depicts the newspaper want ads years later, with column after column seeking applicants for high-paying jobs requiring a minimum of 30,000 hours of video game experience.

Yeah, right. Even in our increasingly computerized world, dexterity with a video joystick is of little value to most employers, and the endless hours spent acquiring it divert children from developing skills that really matter, like writing clearly. To learn to write, it helps to do a lot of reading. Yet many parents fear that the compellingly realistic images in video games threaten to eliminate reading from the American childhood experience.

False alarm. Parents across the land have been thrilled to see their children curled up with the 734-page fourth installment of the Harry Potter series. With an initial print run of 3.8 million copies and millions more on the way, our children will spend more time reading this summer than ever before.

How did the author J. K. Rowling manage to use ink on a printed page to defeat the pull of modern electronic wizardry? Critics may be divided on the literary merits, but young readers really like these books. There have always been good books, however, and quality alone cannot explain the most dazzlingly successful book launch in history.

To understand the phenomenon, we must look to the special properties that make markets for popular culture so different from the markets described in economics textbooks. In textbook accounts, the attractiveness of any given product depends on its style, quality, and other specific attributes. But when books, movies, sporting events, and TV programs are being sold, the choices made by other buyers also matter a great deal.

After all, an important element of reading a book or seeing a movie is the ability to discuss the experience with friends. Once the popularity of a cultural experience reaches a certain threshold, failure to consume it may entail significant social costs. For instance, this past winter, many people could not participate in Monday morning office conversations if they had failed to watch *The Sopranos* the night before. Current sales levels suggest that children who haven't read the latest Potter novel may pay a similar social price.

Markets for popular cultural offerings differ in a second way from ordinary markets, in which the more one consumes of something, the less one is willing to pay to obtain more of it. Even a hungry person, for example, generally would be willing to pay less for a second sandwich than for the first. (This is the law of diminishing marginal utility.) In many markets for popular culture, the actual pattern is the reverse. Early fans of *Saturday Night Live* will recall, for instance, that although the first of John Belushi's Samurai skits was hilarious, it had nothing like the impact of later episodes, when Belushi's mere appearance in his Samurai outfit summoned howls of laughter. Similarly, for many young readers, the more Potter novels they read, the keener is their desire to read another.

Self-reinforcing processes like these give rise to winner-take-all markets, in which small differences between contestants often produce enormous differences in economic reward. In such markets, only a small handful from the initial multitude of contestants end up as big winners, and the question of who those winners will be is often decided by differences that may seem insignificant at the outset.

Winner-take-all markets often encourage furious jockeying for position among contestants. Other authors, perhaps a wastefully large number, will rush to imitate Rowling's success. Most of their efforts may prove fruitless, yet we must be grateful for the explosively self-reinforcing processes that characterize this particular market. Without them, no book could hope to compete with the more spectacular media that vie for our children's attention.

New York Times, July 17, 2000

ONE Thursday afternoon in early 2001, a *Wall Street Journal* reporter called me to discuss winner-take-all markets. When he asked for some examples, I mentioned eBay, the largest online auction service. I told him to imagine he was selling an oriental rug and had to decide whether to list it on eBay or one of the smaller online auction sites.

The advantage of listing it on eBay, I told him, is that because so many more potential buyers would see it there, his odds of finding the right buyer would be considerably higher than on any other site. I went on to explain why I thought eBay would eventually be the only viable online auction site.

The difficulty facing the seller of a specific idiosyncratic object is finding someone who wants to buy something of precisely that description. When more objects are shown to more potential buyers, the odds of finding a good match between buyer and seller go up. This creates an obvious problem for smaller online auction sites, since there may be no positive price they can charge that would make it worth the seller's while to list with them. At the time, eBay was charging a small fixed fee plus something like 4 percent of the listing's final auction price. What price could a smaller auction site charge that would make sellers willing to list there rather than on eBay? Two percent? One percent? Even if the smaller site let sellers list without charge, most sellers would still come out ahead on eBay because its higher traffic level would generally result in a significantly higher winning bid.

The reporter seemed persuaded by my argument and told me that he would probably use the example in his story the following week. On the basis of my analysis of the company's position, I had long been planning to buy stock in eBay but had never gotten around to it. After revealing my penetrating analysis to the reporter, I feared that the company's stock would quickly be bid up to its true value once his story appeared. I knew I had to act quickly but was worried whether it would be ethical to do so, since I had insider knowledge about the forthcoming story that would send eBay's stock price soaring. I discussed the matter with several respected colleagues, who assured me there would be nothing unethical about buying the stock before the story was published.

Being a procrastinator, however, I didn't get around to it. And much to my surprise, eBay's stock price not only failed to rise in the days after the story appeared, it actually fell sharply.

Some months later, I finally got around to buying a block of eBay shares. As I write these words, some seven years later, my shares are trading at about 15 percent less than what I paid for them.

I should have known better. In early 2000, an editor at the *New York Times* asked me to write the following attempt to make sense of the merger between AOL and Time Warner. My analysis in this chapter's final selection, which is hands down the worst piece I've ever written, had persuaded me that buying stock in AOL-TimeWarner would be a smart move. That time I acted quickly. But as events eventually proved, the merger was a dumb idea, and again I lost money. I'll have more to say about the folly of amateur stock picking in Chapter 11.

43. What Was the AOL/Time Warner Merger All About?

Business lore has it that Jack Welch, the chairman of General Electric, called his division heads together at one point during the 1980s and told them to abandon any product that was not one of the top three in its particular market. Pursuing that strategy has made the company one of the most successful conglomerates in American business history.

The same logic helps to explain why an Internet access provider like America Online would want to merge with a traditional media conglomerate like Time Warner. The domain of entertainment and communications, even more than GE's world of manufacturing, has become an environment where success breeds success. The technological imperative is to dominate or perish.

In entertainment and communications, even more than in General Electric's business, many costs are fixed, and the cost of serving additional customers is generally small. The cost of producing a movie or writing Internet access software, for example, is essentially the same whether the product attracts 1 million buyers or 100 million.

So the more customers a company serves, the more cheaply it can sell its product and still make money, which often makes the battle over market share decisive. Investments aimed at enhancing the quality of the product are the most important weapons in that battle.

If Time Warner's Home Box Office bids for star performers or spends more on elaborate special effects for its made-for-TV movies, it can attract more subscribers, yet it will not have to charge each customer a higher price to cover its increased costs. And having a better product would help HBO lure subscribers away from Showtime and Cinemax, reinforcing the initial advantage.

Similar forces govern the contest to provide Internet access. Because many of the biggest costs of delivering Internet service are fixed, the average cost per subscriber declines sharply with the number of subscribers served.

Additional advantages come from having a larger network of customers. When a subscriber wants to check email while traveling abroad, for example, he would prefer not to make an international toll call; only a provider with a dense global network can hope to maintain worldwide local access numbers in cities of small or medium size. Users of the same Internet service also benefit from sharing a platform in common, giving them access to common chat rooms, instant messaging services, and other features.

But why does AOL need Time Warner now that it has already established itself as the dominant global Internet access provider?

The answer is apparent when you compare how much more rapidly you can download information from the Web when using your employer's commercial fiber-optic service than when using the telephone modem system at your home computer, the system that is the backbone of AOL's current service.

America Online is dominant now, but it is unlikely to remain so unless it can find a way to match the service that can be offered to subscribers on high-capacity fiber-optic networks. More and more Internet service is likely to be delivered in the future not through telephone lines but over the high-capacity networks that now deliver cable television.

Time Warner's Roadrunner is one of the largest providers of cable Internet access. With extensive cable TV holdings spanning thirty-three states, Time Warner is ideally positioned to provide the faster Internet connections that consumers now demand.

And since some of what consumers are expected to get over the fast new networks is entertainment, Time Warner stands to benefit by having a partner that is already a powerful Internet presence.

Of course, if the two companies were not to merge, AOL could try to form independent alliances with other cable TV providers. And Time Warner could continue to deploy its cable assets in expanding its own position as an Internet provider. But each of these efforts would be extremely costly and fraught with risk.

In contrast, a merger improves the chances that current stockholders of both companies will end up as winners in the new world where television and the Internet are delivered through the same cables.

Time Warner stockholders who failed to see big profits from the combination of Time and Warner Brothers need to understand that this new merger is not solely about expanding content—the kinds of entertainment offered. It is also about staying alive in a new technological universe.

Consumers are also likely to benefit, since the merger will hasten the arrival of high-speed Internet access to homes. And if the combined company succeeds in its efforts, the quality and availability of Internet access should increase worldwide as well.

Should the Justice Department be worried about this merger? At this point, there seems to be little reason. But if AOL's control of a local cable TV network were an important barrier to competition in delivering Internet services, a simple remedy would be to require the company to lease access to outside providers, much as regulators now require local telephone companies to let others use their wires.

The merger would also provide competition for AT&T, which through its purchase of the cable television network Telecommunications International is now positioned to become one of the largest providers of fast Internet service.

Communications and entertainment markets are classic winner-take-all markets. To remain in the game, companies must play to win.

New York Times, January 11, 2000

10

The Causes and Consequences
of Growing Income Inequality

Imagine that you and two friends are hiking in the Canadian woods when you spot a sparkling object beneath a bush just off the trail. You pick it up and see that it is a large diamond in the rough. A jeweler you trust offers you $900,000 for it. How should this money be apportioned among you and your friends?

Most people say you should share the proceeds equally, which would mean a payment of $300,000 apiece. In attempting to make sense of this response, psychologists say that most people feel a strong commitment to equality as a moral norm.

That commitment, however, is far from absolute. In no country on earth does the government tax 100 percent of each person's income and then distribute the total in equal shares to every citizen. Little wonder, since that would be a recipe for economic disaster. In a country with millions of people, sharing the national income equally would mean that no one would experience any perceptible reduction in his standard of living if he stopped working. Of course, some people would work anyway, because they enjoy their jobs. But many activities besides work are also enjoyable. If a person's income would be the same whether or not he worked, it's safe to assume that most people would choose not to work.

In short, the reason most people think complete equality is an unrealistic goal is that we need to maintain work incentives. Unless individual incomes are linked to work in some clear way, we consign ourselves to lives of abject poverty.

There is a long history of disagreement, however, on how much inequality is necessary to maintain work incentives. There is a similar history of disagreement about whether inequality per se is socially harmful. There has even been disagreement about how much inequality actually exists at any moment.

There is an emerging consensus, however, that inequality has risen substantially in recent decades. The selected columns in this chapter explore the causes and consequences of this change. Many commentators have attributed the increase to a breakdown of competitive forces that has allowed corporate executives and other highly placed insiders to loot their organizations. In the first selection, written in the fall of 2005, I argue that the reverse is more nearly true: rising inequality is primarily a consequence of the fact that markets are much more competitive now than they used to be.

44. Why Has Inequality Been Growing So Rapidly?

Economic inequality has been growing rapidly in the United States, and Congress is about to take steps that will increase it further. How did we get here, and are we wise to continue on this path?

At the end of World War II, income inequality was lower in the United States than at any time since the 1920s. During the ensuing three decades, incomes grew briskly and at about the same rate—

almost 3 percent per year—for households up and down the income ladder.

That pattern began to change in the 1970s. Since 1979, for example, the incomes of families in the bottom 80 percent of the income distribution have grown by less than 1 percent each year, and only households in the top 20 percent have enjoyed income growth comparable to that in the earlier period. For a small group at the very top of the economic ladder, however, incomes have been growing explosively.

For more than twenty-five years, *Business Week* has conducted an annual survey of the earnings of chief executive officers of the largest U.S. corporations. In 1980, those executives earned forty-two times as much as the average American worker, a ratio larger than the corresponding ratios for such countries as Japan and Germany even today. By 2000, however, American CEOs were earning 531 times the average worker's salary. The gains have been even larger for those above CEOs on the income ladder.

With corporate malfeasance much in the news, we know that at least some of the spectacular corporate pay packages were not won on merit. Most of them, however, are a simple consequence of market forces. As local markets have given way to regional, then national, and now global markets, even a few slightly improved executive decisions can now add hundreds of millions of dollars to the bottom line.

More generally, rapid pay growth at the top owes much to the spread of reward structures once confined largely to markets for sports and entertainment. In these winner-take-all markets, small differences in performance often translate into enormous differences in economic reward. Now that we listen mostly to recorded music, the world's best musicians can literally be everywhere at once. The electronic news wire has allowed a small number of syndicated columnists to displace a host of local journalists. And the proliferation of personal computers has enabled a handful of software developers to replace thousands of local tax accountants. Each change has benefited consumers but has also led to greater inequality.

Around the globe, income inequality has been growing for similar reasons. In most countries, public policy has attempted to counter this trend. Not in the United States. With the market's push toward greater inequality already apparent, for example, Congress reduced the top marginal income tax rate from 50 percent to 28 percent during the 1980s.

These tax cuts have increased inequality not only through their direct effects on after-tax income, but also through indirect effects on federal spending policies. Although supply-side economists predicted that the cuts would increase tax revenues by stimulating more than enough income growth to offset the lower rates, this did not happen, and hence the large budget deficits of the 1980s.

Those deficits were eliminated during the Clinton years but have reappeared, larger than ever, under President Bush, who has reduced tax rates on earnings, dividends, and large inheritances. Once the enabling legislation is fully phased in, more than half of the resulting cuts—52.5 percent, according to one recent estimate—will go to the top 5 percent of earners. The nonpartisan Congressional Budget Office now forecasts deficits larger than $300 billion for each of the next six years.

Many proponents of smaller government applaud these deficits, arguing that they will force legislators to cut wasteful spending. As always, however, budget cuts focus not on wasteful programs but on those whose beneficiaries are least able to resist them. Recent proposals by House Republicans would eliminate free school lunches for 40,000 children and food stamps for 225,000 people in working households with children. House Republicans also propose $12 billion in cuts for Medicaid, a program on which 25 percent of American children now rely for access to medical care.

The combined effects of market forces and changes in public policy have clearly made life more difficult for middle- and low-income people. They are working longer hours, saving less, borrowing more, commuting longer distances, and doing without things once considered essential. Personal bankruptcy filings have set new records in each of the last several years. The personal savings rate, always low by international standards, has fallen sharply since the 1980s. It has hovered close to zero since the late 1990s, and in recent months has actually been negative. About 45 million Americans now have no health insurance, 5 million more than in the early 1990s.

Although income inequality has increased sharply in recent decades, it has always been greater here than in other industrial democracies. Can a case be made for it? Many have described inequality as the price we must pay to achieve high rates of economic growth.

The evidence, however, suggests otherwise. As economists Alberto Alesina and Dani Rodrik have found, for example, growth rates across countries are negatively related to the share of national income going to top earners.

Others have portrayed inequality as a necessary condition for socioeconomic mobility, arguing that people who are willing to work hard and play by the rules face a better chance of making it to the top here than in any other country. But here too the evidence suggests otherwise. Even as economic inequality has been rising, social mobility has been declining. According to sociologist David Wright, the probability that a child born to parents in the third quartile of the income distribution would move up into the top quartile was only half as large in 1998 as in 1973. Economist Thomas Hertz has found that children whose parents are in the bottom fifth of the income distribution have only a 7.3 percent chance of making it into the top fifth. In contrast, children born in the top fifth have a 42.3 percent chance of remaining there. Contrary to popular impressions, socioeconomic mobility is now lower in the United Stated than in most other industrialized countries.

Although the market forces that have been producing higher inequality show no signs of abating, Republicans in Congress are now calling for an additional $70 billion in tax cuts aimed largely at high-income families, arguing that because the most prosperous Americans have worked hard, they are entitled to keep a greater portion of their pretax incomes. But tens of millions of less prosperous Americans have worked hard, too. And in winner-take-all markets, examples abound in which some earn thousands of times more than others just as talented and hardworking.

The economist Herbert Stein once said that if something cannot go on forever, it won't. History has repeatedly demonstrated that societies can tolerate income inequality only up to a point, beyond which they rapidly disintegrate. Numerous governments in Latin America have been overthrown largely because of social unrest rooted in income inequality. And in a survey of more than a quarter of a million randomly selected individuals worldwide, economist Robert MacCulloch found that people in countries with high income inequality were much more likely to voice support for violent revolution.

Major social upheavals are sometimes preceded by years or even decades of rising levels of social unrest. If such unrest is currently building in the United States, it remains well hidden. But as recent experience has made clear, social upheavals often occur without warning. Almost no one predicted the fall of the Eastern European governments in 1989. Because revolutions almost always entail important elements of social contagion, even small changes can launch political prairie fires once a tipping point is reached.

As Plutarch wrote almost two thousand years ago, "An imbalance between rich and poor is the oldest and most fatal ailment of all republics." Before the United States succumbs to that ailment, we might want to reconsider the wisdom of policies that widen that already large gap.

Philadelphia Inquirer, November 27, 2005

IN many societies, people in the middle class resent the rich. Not so in the United States. For example, when Robin Leach's television program, *Lifestyles of the Rich and Famous*, was still on the air, millions of eager middle-class viewers tuned in each week. And magazines that chronicle the mansions, yachts, and other dazzling possessions of celebrities have always sold briskly.

American social critics who complain about growing income and wealth inequality are often accused of inciting class warfare or engaging in the politics of envy. In the next selection, written in the closing months of the 2004 presidential election campaign, I suggest that conventional class warfare rhetoric misses the real links between income inequality and living conditions of the middle class.

45. Why Is the Rhetoric of Class Warfare So Rare in America?

If class warfare is being waged in America, my class is clearly winning.
—*Warren E. Buffett, annual letter to Berkshire Hathaway shareholders, March 2004*

As they did in 2000 against Al Gore, Republicans are again deriding Democratic criticism of tax cuts for the wealthy as "class warfare." It's a deft linguistic ploy, for the term was originally used to portray the wealthy as elites who exploited workers unfairly. Many found this rhetoric compelling during the robber baron era, more than a century ago, when employers hired armies of thugs to bust their labor unions.

Today, however, the rhetoric of exploitation falls largely on deaf ears. For despite the recent spate of examples of fortunes amassed by fraud, middle-class voters appear to accept that the current generation of wealthy Americans earned their money not through strong-arm tactics but by offering services that others value highly.

The fact remains, however, that the behavior of the wealthy has been the root cause of a serious economic squeeze confronting the middle class, whose incomes have failed to keep pace with the price of housing, tuition, health insurance, and a host of other basic services during recent decades. Through a chain of events, the increased spending of the top 1 percent, who earned three times as much in 2000 as in 1979, has placed many basic goals out of reach for the median family.

The links in this chain unfold roughly as follows. When the incomes of the wealthy rise, they eventually spend more on houses, cars, clothing, and other goods, just as others do. Upon learning that someone at the top has built a 60,000-square-foot house or purchased a new Ferrari Scaglietti, most of us feel no inclination to alter our own spending.

But among those just below the top, such purchases have an impact. They subtly change the social frame of reference that defines what kinds of houses and cars seem necessary or appropriate. Additional spending by top earners thus leads others just below them to spend more. And when they do so, others just below them are affected in the same way, and so on, all the way down the income ladder.

In short, burgeoning incomes at the top have launched "expenditure cascades" that have ended up squeezing the middle class. An expenditure cascade in housing, for example, helps explain why the median size of a newly constructed house in the United States, which stood at less than 1,600 square feet in 1980, increased to more than 2,100 square feet by 2001. During the same period, the median family's real income increased by less than 15 percent, not nearly enough to comfortably finance a much larger house.

The steep rise in median house prices is one of the most important sources of the middle-class economic squeeze. It is an indirect consequence of the higher incomes and spending of top earners.

A family could escape the squeeze by just buying a smaller house, but that option would entail a significant cost. There is a strong link between the price of a house and the quality of the corresponding neighborhood school. Failure to buy a house near the median price for the area means having to send one's children to below-average schools, a cost that most parents seem unwilling to bear. The upshot is that middle-class families must now work longer hours, borrow more, save less, and commute longer distances in order to continue sending their children to schools of just average quality.

Under the circumstances, it's no mystery that working- and middle-class voters are growing restive. What's surprising, however, is that they remain so free of resentment toward the rich. Indeed, almost two-thirds of low-income survey respondents favor repeal of the estate tax, a step that would benefit only the wealthiest 1 percent. And until recently, few political candidates dared even question the wisdom of large income tax cuts for the wealthy, whose incomes have been growing at record rates.

One reason the middle class feels so little rancor toward the wealthy is that the two groups don't compete directly with each other. As Bertrand Russell once observed, beggars don't envy millionaires. They envy other beggars who are doing just a little better than they are. The fact that Bill Gates might earn an extra billion or build another wing onto his mansion doesn't seem to bother middle-class voters, many of whom enjoy following media accounts of his lifestyle.

And why not? Biologists teach that life is best understood as a competitive struggle for the resources needed to raise families, and for middle-class voters, the rivals who matter are not people like Bill Gates. In the quest for a better job or a house in a better school district, it's the people most like ourselves who really count. From the perspective of a middle-class voter struggling to get ahead, fretting about the good fortune of the rich is a complete distraction.

Even so, the expenditure cascade launched by top earners has placed a real burden on middle- and low-income families. This is not to say that top earners have done anything wrong. Certainly it was not their intent to cause trouble for those below. Yet the runaway prosperity they've enjoyed in recent decades has imposed significant tangible costs on the middle class.

That the link between spending at the top and the squeeze on the middle class is indirect may explain why there is so little resentment toward the rich, but those who evaluate economic policies cannot ignore it.

Recently enacted federal tax legislation will steer almost $700 billion in tax reductions to the wealthiest 1 percent during the next decade. In response, these people will build still bigger mansions and buy still more expensive cars. And a new round of expenditure cascades will put additional financial pressure on the middle class.

To question the wisdom of tax cuts for the wealthy is not to issue a battle call for class warfare. Repealing those cuts would not only alleviate the economic squeeze on families in the middle, it also might even make life more enjoyable for the wealthy. After all, managing a 60,000-square-foot mansion is a major headache. If fewer people built houses that large, fewer still would feel any desire to own one.

Philadelphia Inquirer, September 12, 2004

ALTHOUGH most people in the middle class seem disinclined to express moral outrage over the lavish expenditures of the very wealthy, many social critics display no such reluctance. Such outrage, however, betrays a certain lack of perspective. The plain fact is that people at every income level tend to spend in accordance with their income. When the poor receive additional money they spend it. The same is true of middle- and high-income people. It may seem only natural to characterize the purchases of wealthy Americans as frivolous, but to the billions of people who currently earn less than $2 per day, the purchases of middle-income Americans would seem even more frivolous. The standards that define what is considered appropriate or desirable are always local. If people in the middle class have good reason to think they aren't spending frivolously, so do people who are wealthy.

The following selection originally appeared in the *New York Times Magazine* in October 2000, the height of the dot-com bubble. In it, I describe the bemused reactions of a friend who grew up in a middle-income family in the Midwest and then found herself suddenly wealthy in Silicon Valley.

46. Does Having Rich Neighbors Make You Feel Poor?

Most of us are taught from an early age not to worry about how the possessions of others compare with our own, and we seem to recognize the soundness of this advice. There will always be people with more, and focusing on that is a recipe for misery. So if asked whether we fret about the size of our neighbor's house or the kind of cars they drive, most of us would insist we do not.

Put the question another way, however, and we seem a little less certain. Consider a choice between these two worlds:

World A: You earn $110,000 per year; others earn $200,000.

World B: You earn $100,000 per year; others earn $85,000.

The income figures represent real purchasing power. Your income in World A would command a house 10 percent larger than the one you could afford in World B, 10 percent more restaurant dinners, and so on. By choosing World B, you'd give up a small amount of absolute income in return for a large increase in relative income.

So which would you pick? A majority of Americans, it turns out, choose World B.

Why would we accept the lower pay? One possibility, of course, is that we envy our neighbors' possessions more than we feel comfortable admitting. But there's an alternative explanation, one that works even if we're really not much concerned about keeping up with the Joneses.

This alternative account rests on the idea that to function effectively in complex social environments, we need ways to evaluate how we're doing and make judgments about how best to adapt to changing environments. Such judgments almost always depend heavily on how we're doing relative to others in the same local environment. Suppose your daughter just got a D on her first exam at Stanford. She could console herself with the notion that her performance would have earned a much higher grade had she gone to a junior college close to home, but she probably won't see it that way. She's likely to be upset. The low grade tells her something important. She needs to work harder, and being upset will prod her to do so.

Similar contextual forces mold our assessment of the things we own. For example, as Adam Smith observed in *Wealth of Nations,* local standards define how much people must spend on clothing if they are to appear in public "without shame." In eighteenth-century Scotland, he wrote, even the lowliest workers needed shirts made of linen, since the inability to afford a shirt of that quality generally signified indolence, incompetence, or worse.

Fashions have of course evolved since Smith's day, but his insight remains valid. And the stakes now are greater than ever. In the midst of the longest sustained economic boom in history, many American families are experiencing an unprecedented sense of impoverishment. They feel poorer not just because of the growing earnings gap between the rich and others, but also because of a newer phenomenon: in this media-dominated age, we're far more aware than we've ever been of the wealth that surrounds us. This new economic climate has profoundly changed how we live and how we spend our money.

I have a friend in California who could almost be mistaken for a typical American. She lives with her husband and young daughter, and she wants a bigger house, because their current one lacks a basement and they want more storage space. She worries about the quality of public schools and wouldn't mind paying higher taxes if something could be done to improve them. And like millions of others, she considers herself a frugal, environmentally sensitive person.

In other ways, my friend is less typical, and context has nearly everything to do with it. Context explains why she gets a weekly massage and a pedicure at least once a month, things she hardly ever did before. Context explains why she always flies first class, after half a lifetime of coach. Context explains why she and her husband recently bought an $80,000 convertible, and why they buy tens of thousands of dollars worth of new electronic equipment each year. Most of all, context explains why they live in a house that cost them $2 million.

My friend, you see, lives in Los Altos, one of Silicon Valley's wealthiest suburbs, where the standards are vastly different from those in the Midwest, where she grew up. Many of her neighbors are rich on a scale that most of us find difficult to comprehend. Although my friend and her husband can easily afford their current lifestyle, they're also a bit puzzled by it. "Ten years ago," she says, "there's no way I'd have imagined ourselves spending as much as we do today. But living here, things are different." In Los Altos, a $2 million, 3,500-square-foot house is unremarkable, and few neighbors would find it strange that my friend is considering a bigger one. "I always wanted to live in a big house with lots of space," she says. "I don't know how large. I guess maybe double what we have."

Her experience differs in degree, though not in kind, from those of millions of other American families during the current boom. In the abstract, many of these families continue to embrace simple, unostentatious modes of living. Yet they find their sense of what they need pushed inexorably higher by the rapidly escalating consumption all around them.

In large measure, we spend more because we have more. There are now 590,000 American households worth $5 million or more. And by 2004, according to the Spectrem Group, their ranks will swell to 3.9 million.

These numbers are so big they cover up a simple fact: the vast majority of us still aren't rich. And while much is made of how the wealthy have segregated themselves from mainstream society—living in gated communities, sending their kids to private schools—they are all around us. Even my small university-dominated city, which sits squarely within the vast economic sinkhole that is upstate New York, now has its own booming stratum of biotech and dot-com multimillionaires. If we don't know these people directly, we know others who know them. Servicing the wealthy has become one of the fastest-growing employment sectors, bringing the rich into daily contact with millions of ordinary Americans. We clean their houses, mow their lawns, teach their kids French, do their taxes. More than ever, the rich have become part of our local context, nudging upward our sense of what is required to live comfortably and securely.

Add to that the long-standing media fixation on money. Television shows and magazines have always presented the rich as objects of fascination but have usually portrayed their lives as exotic and fanciful, as opposed to those of ordinary people. That has changed. One can scarcely get through a magazine these days, for example, without encountering a report that $45,000 Patek Philippe wristwatches and $25 million Feadship yachts are available only on back order. On Sunday football telecasts, ads for Heineken and BMW have displaced those for Miller Lite and Ford pickups, even though the same people, more or less, are watching.

No matter how much the media focus on the extraordinarily wealthy, however, the strongest contextual influences on how we spend remain the ones closest to home. H. L. Mencken once defined a wealthy man as one who earns $100 a year more than his wife's sister's husband. A recent study found striking support for Mencken's definition. Economists David Neumark and Andrew Postlewaite examined the behavior of a large sample of pairs of American sisters, each containing a sister who did not work outside the home. The authors' goal was to learn what factors might influence the other sister to seek paid employment. They rounded up all the things that are supposed to affect the decision to work—the unemployment rate in the local labor market, the wage rate, education. All of these factors had some impact, but relative income was the most powerful. A woman in their sample was 16 to 25 percent more likely to seek paid employment if her sister's husband earned more than her own.

The ever widening wealth and income gap between the rich and everybody else has meant that a growing number of Americans now find themselves in the role of the impoverished in-law. Middle-income families, whose inflation-adjusted incomes are no higher now than in the 1970s, have been saving at much lower rates than before, indeed, even at negative rates for much of last year. They're also carrying record levels of credit card debt and other loans, going without health insurance and filing for bankruptcy at several times the rate of the early 1980s. In short, middle-income families are experiencing unprecedented levels of economic distress, largely because they are trying to keep up with a living standard they cannot afford.

Financial distress in the middle class is an important problem, and social critics have been vigilant in their search for villains. Writers from the "personal responsibility" movement, for example, denounce those they consider too weak-willed to resist the influence of other people's spending. In their view, middle-class families should just spend less and stop complaining. Other critics, notably those of the "voluntary simplicity" school, express contempt for the buyers of the McMansions springing up all around us. What these judgments ignore is how context shapes our spending decisions at all levels of the economy, and at all standards of taste.

As a young man, I served for two years as a Peace Corps volunteer in Nepal. The one-room house I lived in had no plumbing or electricity, and its thatched roof leaked during heavy rains. At no time, however, did I feel it was unsatisfactory in any way. Yet I could not live in that same house in the United States, even in the poorest neighborhood, without experiencing a profound sense of humiliation. If I had to go into debt to escape that experience, I certainly would.

As it happens, I live in a comfortable American middle-class house. But social critics might do well to reflect on how such a house would strike the median earner on planet earth. If a friend from my village in Nepal saw our house, he'd think I'd taken leave of my senses. Why, he'd wonder, would a family of four possibly need a house with three and a half bathrooms?

The plain fact is that the kind of house people feel they need depends on the kind of house that others around them have. Living in a house priced well below average often means living in a relatively dangerous neighborhood or sending your child to a below-average school. Wanting to avoid these penalties is totally normal.

The new economic climate has led us to spend more, borrow more, and save less. These are symptoms of a social problem, no question about it. But the feelings that give rise to this problem are no more blameworthy than those of a student who's upset about getting a D on an exam.

New York Times Magazine, October 15, 2000

THE brain's perception systems are less sensitive to the absolute levels of light, sound, and other stimuli than to changes in those levels. Visual systems, for example, are better at detecting objects in motion than objects at rest, which explains why many animals instinctively freeze when they confront a predator rather than attempt to flee. By the same token, auditory systems are less sensitive to absolute sound levels than to changes in those levels, which explains why people who have fallen asleep with the television on often awaken with a start when someone turns it off.

The same phenomenon helps explain the timing of social commentary. Although the rich have always spent much more than others, little was said about that fact during the 1950s and 1960s. During those years, incomes were growing about 3 percent a year for families up and down the income ladder. Then, as now, the rich lived in larger houses than the middle class. But because the proportional gap in house size wasn't changing, it attracted little notice. Since the 1970s, however, middle-income families have seen their income stagnate while the income of the rich has grown faster than ever before. The gap between what the rich and others buy has thus been changing rapidly. It is not surprising, then, that so much has been written in recent years about the lavish spending of the rich. The following selection, which originally appeared in the *Washington Post* in January 1999, was adapted from my book *Luxury Fever,* published that year.

47. What Caused the Luxury Spending Boom?

The propane grill I bought in the mid-1980s has been on a downhill slide for several years. Even if I found someone who could upgrade it, the cost would surely exceed the $89.95 I originally paid for it. Reluctantly, I find myself in the market for a new one.

If you have shopped for a grill recently, you know that the array of choices is profoundly different from ten years ago. I vaguely remember seeing some models then with built-in storage cabinets and shelf extensions on either side. But even with these frills, the most you could spend was a few hundred dollars. There was nothing—absolutely nothing—like the Viking Frontgate professional grill.

Powered by either natural gas or propane, it comes with an infrared rotisserie that can slowly broil two twenty-pound turkeys to perfection as you cook hamburgers for forty guests on its 828-square-inch grilling surface. On a side platform are two ancillary range-top burners. Unlike the standard burners on your kitchen stove, which generate 7,500 BTUs, these generate 15,000 BTUs, a capability primarily useful for the flash stir-frying of some ethnic cuisines and for bringing large cauldrons of water to a boil more quickly. With its foldout work spaces fully extended, it measures more than seven feet across.

The Frontgate catalog's price for the Viking grill, not including shipping and handling, is $5,000. Of course, many cheaper models are also available. For chefs who feel they can get by with an eighteen-by-twenty-four-inch grilling surface and only one ancillary burner, Frontgate offers a $1,140 Viking model that delivers "professional results at a great value." But even that stripped-down model costs considerably more than most of us would have dreamed of spending a mere decade ago.

The real significance of the $5,000 grill, for most of us, is that it makes buying a $1,000 unit seem almost frugal. As more people buy these up-market grills, the frame of reference that defines what the rest of us consider an acceptable price will inevitably continue to shift. In this age of prosperity, I could easily spend $1,000 on a new grill tomorrow and few people would think I had done anything strange. But far more unsettling is the possibility that it wouldn't occur to me that there was anything strange about spending $1,000 to replace a $90 gas grill.

The evolution of spending patterns in the gas grill industry is part of a broader change that has taken place in recent decades. We are in the grip of a luxury fever that rivals the spectacular excesses of the Gilded Age of a century ago. But unlike that earlier period, which was dominated by a small number of families with enormous wealth, our current consumption boom involves a vastly larger number of people all along the economic spectrum.

Although it is the mansions of the superrich that attract attention—homes of 15,000, 20,000, even 40,000 square feet—the more newsworthy fact is that the area of the average house built in the United States is now more than twice what it was in the 1970s. And although it is the $250,000 sticker price of the sleek twelve-cylinder Lamborghini Diablo that prompts the finger wagging of social critics, the more telling observation is that the average price of an automobile sold in the United States now exceeds $22,000, up more than 75 percent from just a decade earlier.

No matter where you stand on the income scale, no matter how little you feel you are influenced by what others do, you cannot escape the effects of this spending spree. Among other things, it affects how much you spend for birthday gifts, the price you pay to live in a neighborhood with a good school, the kinds of sneakers your children demand, the cost of the universities you want them to attend, or the price of the suit you buy to wear to an interview for a better job.

It is this cascading effect that is new and troubling. The real question is whether anything practical can be done about it. My case for change (more on that later) rests not at all on the social critic's claim that luxury consumption is self-indulgent or decadent, but on detailed and persuasive scientific evidence that if we alter some of the incentives that are fueling consumption, all of us can expect to live more satisfying lives.

No government report charts the luxury boom. To get a feel of it, we must compose a picture from assorted bits and pieces. Sales of wristwatches that sell for at least $2,000 rose 13 percent in 1997, to $1.1 billion. Luxury cars (those costing more than $30,000 in 1996 dollars) accounted for about 12 percent of all vehicles sold in the United States in 1996, up from 7 percent a decade earlier. Total wine consumption in the United States is down slightly from its 1986 peak, but sales of ultrapremium wines have grown by 23 percent a year since 1980.

At one level, the recent upgrades in what we buy might seem a benign symptom of the fact that we are more productive, and hence richer, than ever before. But there is a dark side to our current spending patterns. Whereas those at the top of the economic heap have done spectacularly well, the median American family has gained virtually no ground at all during the past two decades, and the earnings of those in the bottom fifth have actually declined more than 10 percent in purchasing power.

Middle- and low-income families have thus had to finance their higher spending by a lower rate of savings and sharply rising debt. In the process, our personal savings rate, which has always been much smaller than that of any other industrial nation, has steadily fallen. One in seventy American families filed for bankruptcy last year.

Even for those who can easily afford today's luxury offerings, there has been a price to pay. All of us, rich and poor alike, are spending more time at the office and taking shorter vacations; we are spending less time with our families and friends; and we have less time for sleep, exercise, travel, reading, and other activities that help maintain body and soul. Because of our declining savings rate, our economic growth rate has slowed, and a rising number of families feel apprehensive about their ability to maintain their living standard during retirement.

Meanwhile, our highways, bridges, water supply systems, and other parts of our public infrastructure are deteriorating. Our parks and streets are becoming more congested. Poverty and drug abuse continue to plague many of our cities. A growing percentage of middle- and upper-income families seek refuge behind the walls of gated residential communities. Citing budget deficits, many community libraries have cut back their hours.

A century hence, those who read the history of our time will be puzzled by some of our choices during this time of economic boom, as well as by our arguments for slashing government budgets and refusing to finance so many useful projects. When our spending on luxury goods is growing four times as fast as overall spending and national income is now more than $8 trillion a year—an average of almost $30,000 for every man, woman, and child—it is peculiar to say we "can't afford" to repair our crumbling infrastructure or spend more time with friends and family. Simply by reducing the rate of growth in luxury consumption, we could afford to do all these things and more.

Social critics in the past have relied mainly on their own personal prejudices about how we might best spend our money. But a large body of scientific literature suggests our recent spending patterns have not served us well. Careful studies show, for example, that when everyone acquires bigger houses and more expensive automobiles, the new higher standards quickly become the norm, with the result that these expenditures yield little lasting satisfaction.

Other evidence suggests, however, that the same resources could have been used in ways that would bring permanent increases in health and happiness. The time required to earn the money to pay for a larger house, for instance, could be freed up for family and friends, exercise, or longer vacations. For want of a better term, we may call this kind of spending "inconspicuous consumption."

People who spend more on inconspicuous consumption are more likely to describe themselves as happy. They are less likely to become involved in disputes at work. They are less likely to seek psychological counseling or to attempt suicide. And they are less likely to become ill or die in any given year.

If we would be happier and healthier working shorter hours and spending more time with our families, even though that would mean living in smaller houses and buying less expensive cars, why don't we just do it? A plausible explanation is at hand once we recognize that our evaluations of virtually everything—from the weather to our material standards of living—are highly dependent on context.

If you ask people in Havana on a 60 degree day in November whether it's cold outside, they'll think you're asking a stupid question. Of course it's cold! But ask the same question in Montreal on a 60 degree day in March, and people there will also wonder about your intelligence. And yet their answer would be precisely the opposite of what people in Havana said.

A similar logic governs the evaluation of material living standards. Is a twelve-foot by twelve-foot master bedroom big enough? My wife and I—upper-middle-class American professionals whose current bedroom is that size—have decided it isn't. That's why a contractor's crew will arrive tomorrow morning to start on an expansion.

If we lived in Tokyo, however, it never would have occurred to us to bear this expense and inconvenience. There, a bedroom like ours would have seemed an embarrassingly large sleeping space, and any discussions we had with contractors would likely have involved partitioning it rather than expanding it.

Adam Smith's celebrated invisible hand—the economic theory that society as a whole does best when people selfishly pursue their own interests in the open marketplace—works only when each person's choices have no negative consequences for others. But when context matters, even the most ordinary individual spending choices affect others.

If I buy a six-thousand-pound sport utility vehicle, I increase the likelihood that others driving a lighter car will die in a traffic accident; in the process, I create an incentive for them to buy a heavier vehicle than they otherwise would have chosen. If I buy a custom-tailored suit for a job interview, I reduce the likelihood that others will land the same job; in the process, I create an incentive for them to spend more on their own suits. When I stay an extra hour at the office each day, I increase my chances for promotion; in the process, I reduce the promotion prospects of others, and thereby create an incentive for them to work longer hours than they otherwise would have chosen. And by deciding to build a larger bedroom, I increase, however slightly, the odds that my neighbors will do likewise. In these ways, our individual spending decisions are the seeds that gave rise to our current luxury fever.

In short, the incentives that guide individual spending decisions are much like those that generate military arms races. Spending less would be better, but only if everyone did it.

Continued carping by social critics has not, and will not, make this happen. Indeed, efforts to curb conspicuous consumption have failed—because we have failed to account properly for the role of context and incentives in economic decisions. If we want to get off the consumption treadmill, we must alter the incentives that led us to spend so much in the first place.

We can do this in a powerful yet unintrusive way by scrapping our current income tax in favor of a more steeply progressive consumption tax. Each family would pay tax not on its income but on its total spending, as measured by the simple difference between its annual income and its annual savings.

Because the rich save and invest so much more than the poor, fairness would require that tax rates on the highest spenders be significantly higher than the current top tax rates on incomes. But even if tax rates were set to raise no more total revenue than under the current system, a consumption tax would have a profound effect on specific purchase decisions.

Consider the choice between a Porsche 911 Turbo ($105,000) and a Ferrari 456 GT ($207,000). The Ferrari buyer is currently willing to spend $102,000 more for his top-of-the-line purchase. But with a top rate on taxable consumption of, say, 70 percent, the effective premium to buy the Ferrari would be more than $173,000.

Because the consumption tax offers an exemption for savings, the Ferrari buyer would have a strong incentive to invest a little more in the stock market and spend a little less on his car. If he buys the Porsche, his outlay—including the tax—will be $178,000. In return, he gets a car that performs just as well as the Ferrari and, assuming others have responded similarly, just as rare. The tax preserves the aficionado's ability to indulge his passion for sports cars while increasing his savings.

This change in incentives, if phased in gradually, would sharply curb the recent explosive growth of spending on luxury goods. Ironically, it would do so without any sacrifice in satisfaction by luxury goods buyers, since what counts is not absolute spending on these goods but relative spending. As the biggest spenders began to save more, the consumption standards that the rest of us feel compelled to meet would relax as well, freeing up resources that could be put to far better uses.

A cautious reading of the evidence suggests that we could spend one-third less on consumption—roughly $2 trillion per year—and suffer no significant reduction in satisfaction. Savings of that magnitude could help pay for restoring our infrastructure, for cleaner air and water, and a variety of other things.

Moreover, the consumption tax would not erode our cherished political freedoms. On the contrary, by increasing the extent to which private interests coincide with social interests, it would actually help breathe new life into Adam Smith's invisible hand, thereby increasing the extent to which we can rely on private markets to allocate goods and services efficiently.

If the progressive consumption tax is such a great idea, why don't we already have one? In a tax-phobic country such as ours, this tax would be a difficult platform for a politician to run on, even though it would in fact yield gains for everyone. But even if current distractions were to end and advocates of the progressive consumption tax did step forward, we would need months, perhaps years, of focused debate to build consensus for changing the system. In the meantime, the luxury spending boom will continue apace.

Washington Post, January 24, 1999

HIGHER spending by top earners launches expenditure cascades that put additional pressure on middle-class families to spend more, even though their income may not have risen. But how can a family spend more without earning more? The answer is that there are multiple ways of trying to make ends meet. Families can save less or borrow more. And they have been doing both. They can also work longer hours. And in many European countries, there is evidence for that pattern also.

Another option for families struggling to keep up is to move farther from the center of economic activity, where housing prices are lower, and then endure longer commutes to work. In the next selection, I spell out how tax cuts for the wealthy cause average commute times to lengthen.

48. How Do Tax Cuts Worsen Traffic Jams?

Traffic jams are a nuisance. But they are more than that. Studies have shown that compared with people who walk or take public transportation to work, people who face protracted commutes in heavy traffic are more likely to experience high blood pressure. They have more frequent disputes with their coworkers and families. They suffer more frequent and more serious illnesses. And they are more likely to experience premature death.

Traffic jams are also getting much worse. A recent study by Texas A&M University, for example, reported that Americans spent three times as many hours stalled in traffic in 1999 as they did in 1982.

Although increased traffic congestion stems from many familiar causes (like population growth, cheap gasoline prices, increased urban sprawl, and failure to invest in public transport), it is also the result of another factor that has received little attention—increased inequality in income and wealth.

The basic mechanism at work is something I call the Aspen effect. Wealthy residents have long since bid up real estate prices in Aspen and other exclusive resort communities to levels that virtually exclude middle- and low-income families. Most of the people who provide services in these communities—teachers, policemen, firemen, laundry and restaurant workers—must therefore commute, often at considerable distance. As a result, all roads into Aspen are clogged morning and night with commuters, many of whom come from several hours away. "Greater Aspen" now has a radius of more than fifty miles!

Traffic congestion has been getting worse in part because during the past twenty years much of the United States has become more like greater Aspen. Since 1980, the inflation-adjusted income of the top 1 percent of families has more than doubled, while the corresponding growth for the median family has been less than 10 percent. During that same period, families in the bottom 20 percent actually saw their income fall in real terms.

As a result of these changes, residential patterns have become much more stratified by income. The effect has been more pronounced in some communities (the San Francisco peninsula, Austin, and Seattle) than others (Chicago, Philadelphia). But the direction of change has been the same almost everywhere, and it has contributed to the rise in traffic delays.

The current policy agenda in Washington not only promises little relief for harried commuters but is likely to make matters worse. Start with the tax cut. In the proposed $1.35 trillion reduction,

40 percent of the benefits would go to families in the top 5 percent. By making the income gap greater than it is already, this measure is likely to push low- and middle-income families even farther from their jobs, thus increasing their commutes. Granted, the Aspen effect probably would not make anyone's list of the ten most important reasons for opposing the tax cut. But it's yet another drawback to the Bush proposal.

Tax cuts would also put more pressure on already overcommitted government budgets, making it all but impossible to launch significant new urban transit programs in the next decade. And prospects for curtailing traffic congestion are further dimmed by the Bush administration's denial of any legitimate national interest in energy conservation. "The American way of life is a blessed one, and we have a bounty of resources in this country," said Ari Fleischer, the president's spokesman. "The American people's use of energy is a reflection of the strength of our economy, of the way of life that the American people have come to enjoy."

Our country does have a bounty of resources, but that doesn't eliminate the need to make intelligent decisions about how to use them. Traffic jams make life miserable for the rich, as well as for low- and middle-income families. They are neither an essential component of the good life nor inevitable. They can be greatly curtailed by smart public policy.

New York Times, May 11, 2001

IN November 1998, an editor for the *New York Times* op-ed page asked me to write a piece on what kinds of Christmas gifts the wealthy were buying for their children. I decided the best way to find out was to pose as a wealthy shopper and ask up-market Manhattan retailers for advice. I don't own an expensive suit, but I do own a pair of good shoes, which I wore with an old pair of jeans as I made my rounds one Saturday. The last selection in this chapter is based on my field notes from those visits.

49. Hey, Timmy, How Much Was That Range Rover?

So, what are people with real money buying for their ten-year-olds this Christmas? Put this question to a personal shopper at FAO Schwarz and she'll promptly escort you to a glass-walled inner sanctum on the second floor. There, on display or in a limited-edition catalog, you'll see life-size reproductions of Darth Vader and other Star Wars characters for $5,000 and up, a castle bed with loft for $30,000, and a hand-carved carousel from Germany for $75,000.

But by far the hottest item this season is a Range Rover a quarter the size of the real thing. With leather upholstery and an AM-FM cassette stereo, it is powered by a five-horsepower gasoline engine and has a top speed of twenty miles per hour.

They're selling fast, but you can still take immediate delivery for $18,500, slightly more than the sticker price of a Honda Accord.

Value-conscious shoppers might find that a bit much to pay for a toy car with a lawn mower engine. But they would be missing the point. Forget Furby, this is a serious toy! Even an investment banker's ten-year-old would be thrilled to get one.

Over-the-top spending for kids isn't new. Nor is the junior Rover the most egregious instance. We read, for example, of Manhattan coming-of-age celebrations that cost $250,000, not counting the optional $20,000 six-minute Grucci fireworks display.

But the most expensive gifts for children now have much higher price tags than they used to, which is also true of the gifts exchanged by their up-market parents. When a recent Neiman Marcus Christmas catalog offered the new Jaguar convertible at $80,000, the entire seventy-vehicle inventory was snapped up within hours.

America's new luxury fever is driven by a sharply increased concentration of income and wealth. By one measure, the top 1 percent of earners have captured almost 80 percent of all earnings growth since 1979. If trends continue as expected and are reinforced by enactment of flat-tax proposals that would cut rates on top earners by half, the hottest selling toy car will soon be not the junior Rover but FAO Schwarz's miniature Ferrari, which currently sells for $40,000.

Obviously adults have the right to spend their income however they please. Yet few would insist that these purchases constitute the most fruitful use of this money. Indeed, persuasive scientific evidence suggests that when everyone gets more expensive and elaborate toys, no one is any happier than before.

So why do parents buy such things? The problem is that gift giving is like an arms race: spending less would be better, but only if everybody did it.

The moral outrage of social critics won't make that happen. But a one-line amendment to the federal tax code could. Switching from our current progressive income tax to a more steeply progressive consumption tax would provide powerful incentives to save and invest money that would otherwise be spent on high-end toys.

Such a tax would be easy to administer. A family would pay tax on its total consumption, defined simply as the difference between what it earned (as currently reported to the Internal Revenue Service) and what it saved. The tax rate on the highest spenders would have to be higher than it is now, to allow for the fact that the rich save much more than others. Everyone's tax burden would be roughly the same as before.

But each family's incentive to buy high-end toys would be changed profoundly. If the additional consumption of top spenders were taxed at a rate of, say, 70 percent, the junior Rover's effective price would jump almost $13,000. (The check to FAO Schwarz would remain the same, but parents who bought the car would pay almost $13,000 more in taxes at the end of the year than if they had saved the money instead.)

Just as high real estate prices have induced Manhattan's wealthy to choose smaller dwellings than their counterparts in other cities, this change would lead many to choose less expensive toys and shelter the savings in tax-free mutual funds. As more families followed that course, the standard that defines an acceptable toy would shift. Before long, less expensive toys would acquire the same cachet as the more expensive models they displaced.

This pattern would be repeated all the way down the income ladder, a welcome development at a time when one in seventy American families files for bankruptcy each year. Best of all, it would exact no price in enjoyment, since what counts is not absolute spending on toys but relative spending.

Of course, a steeply progressive consumption tax would also affect other purchase decisions. Many parents might forgo their own $80,000 Range Rovers, choosing $50,000 BMWs instead. Here too we could expect similar savings in other income classes.

Before we saw Tim Robbins driving a Range Rover in Robert Altman's film *The Player* in 1992, only a handful of us had any idea what a Rover even was, much less that we needed one to signal our economic success. A return to that innocent condition would not injure us, and the money thus saved could be put to far more urgent uses. Once our savings rates got healthier, we might even consider—dare I say it—a slight increase in total tax revenue for things that really matter. Just a few painless retrenchments would repair the leaky roofs and broken toilets in the overcrowded, understaffed elementary schools five miles north of the FAO Schwarz showroom.

Not to worry, though, Timmy. None of this will happen anytime soon.

New York Times, December 22, 1998

11

Borrowing, Saving, and Investing

onsumer spending makes up roughly two-thirds of total spending for the economy as a whole, with most of the rest consisting of government and business investment spending. So it's difficult to design sensible economic policy or forecast economic activity accurately without a clear understanding of the forces that drive consumer behavior. As I suggested in my column about the strange disappearance of James Duesenberry (Chapter 4), however, the recent track record of traditional economic theories of consumer behavior has been disappointing. And since the only two things a family can do with its income is spend it or save it, failure to understand the forces that drive consumption also implies failure to understand the forces that drive savings.

That traditional economic models have fallen short in these areas is not surprising. These models imagine rational consumers who plan their lifetime consumption trajectories to maximize their total life satisfaction. But real people often seem to find it difficult to compute what such a plan would require; and even when they are able to formulate a reasonable plan, they often find it difficult to execute.

The behavioral economics revolution has done much to advance our understanding of consumption and savings. The selected columns in this chapter discuss the various discrepancies we observe between what traditional models predict and what people actually do. With a better understanding of the forces that drive consumption, we can better predict how people will respond to changes in the economic environment. Given the importance of consumption in total spending, that means we can better predict where the overall economy is headed.

Traditional economic theories have not supplied a convincing account for the recent sharp decline in the American household savings rate. During the 1980s, American households on average saved almost 10 percent of their income. In the intervening years, the savings rate has dropped steadily toward zero, occasionally dipping into negative territory as households employed home equity loans and credit card debt to spend more than they earned.

Shortly after being sworn in for his second term in office, George W. Bush led an intense campaign to persuade voters to support his proposal to privatize the nation's Social Security system. In the end, this effort attracted little support. That was a good thing, in my view, because the Bush proposal was flawed in fundamental ways. At its core, however, it contained an important insight. The Social Security system is a pay-as-you-go program, not a savings program. Payroll taxes are levied on workers, and the receipts are mailed out as checks to retirees. This method of pension finance gets money into the hands of retirees but fails to take advantage of the miracle of compound interest.

IN this chapter's first selection, written in the midst of the Bush privatization campaign, I describe why compound interest constitutes such a valuable opportunity and speculate about why families may need to act collectively to take full advantage of it.

50. Why Do Americans Save So Little?

The single-cell paramecium is about the size of the period at the end of this sentence. In many species, mature cells divide daily into two daughter cells. In classrooms around the world, this feature has made the paramecium a favorite vehicle for illustrating the miracle of compound interest.

Left unchecked for sixty-four days, a single paramecium would become a colony of 9,223,400,000,000,000,000 members. Since 125 paramecia lined up shoulder to shoulder would span about an inch, this means a string spanning more than 1,164,600,000,000 miles— over 6,000 round trips between the earth and sun.

The story is less dramatic, of course, for growth rates much smaller than the paramecium's. Even with relatively small growth rates, however, the gains are impressive. Money invested at 7 percent interest, for example, will double every ten years, which means that $1,000 deposited at that rate by Benjamin Franklin in the late 1700s would be worth more than $3 trillion today. The same $1,000 invested in 1945 would be worth more than $64,000.

Given the miracle of compound interest, our ability to invest at even modest rates of return represents an extraordinary opportunity. Yet Americans have largely squandered it. Our savings rate, always low by international standards, has fallen sharply in recent decades.

Almost a fifth of American adults have net worth of zero or less. Even more troubling, it is now common for families to pay $1,800 and more in annual interest on revolving credit card balances. Those families experience the miracle of compound interest in reverse.

The savings shortfall threatens not just those who face retrenchment in retirement living standards, but also the country's economic prosperity. With little of Americans' own savings to finance domestic investment, the United States has been borrowing more than $600 billion each year from foreigners.

The mushrooming foreign debt, now almost one-fourth of gross domestic product, has already weakened the dollar and threatens far more serious harm.

Why do Americans save so little? Lack of self-discipline is one reason. If that were the only problem, families could solve it by simply committing a portion of each year's income growth into a payroll savings account, placing it out of temptation's reach.

But the savings shortfall also stems from a second source, one less amenable to this solution. The basic idea is captured in the following thought experiment:

If you were society's median earner, which option would you prefer?

1. You save enough to support a comfortable standard of living in retirement, but your children attend a school whose students score in the 20th percentile on standardized tests in reading and math.

2. You save too little to support a comfortable standard of living in retirement, but your children attend a school whose students score in the 50th percentile on those tests.

It is an unpleasant choice, to be sure, but most people say they would pick the second option.

Because the concept of a "good" school is relative, this thought experiment captures an essential element of the savings decision confronting most families. If others bid for houses in better school districts, failure to do likewise will often consign one's children to inferior schools. Yet no matter how much each family spends, half of all children must attend schools in the bottom half.

The savings decision thus resembles the collective action problem inherent in a military arms race. Each nation knows that it would be better if everyone spent less on arms. Yet if others keep spending, it is too dangerous not to follow suit. Curtailing an arms race requires an enforceable agreement. Similarly, unless all families can bind themselves to save more, those who do so unilaterally risk having to send their children to inferior schools.

People in other countries also face temptation and collective action problems. Why do they save more than we do? One explanation is that both problems are made worse by income disparities, which have widened much faster in this country than elsewhere.

A collective agreement that each family save a portion of its income growth each year would attack both sources of the savings shortfall. Such an agreement might specify that one-third of income growth be diverted into savings until a target savings rate—say, 12 percent of income—was achieved. A family whose income did not rise in a given year would be exempt from the agreement.

Such an agreement would put the magic of compound interest to work for retirement savings, a benefit that the current Social Security system completely misses. Most of the money currently taken from workers in payroll taxes gathers no interest in the decades before their retirement. Instead, it is paid directly to current retirees, who spend it on rent and food. We have a pay-as-we-go system because the program was started in the Great Depression, when there was no money to create a fully financed system.

The good news is that Americans now have ample wealth to support such a system. Some have praised President Bush's proposal to privatize Social Security as a move that will create a fully financed program of retirement savings. It is no such thing. Under his proposal, the transition to private accounts is to be financed with borrowed money. The interest earned on private accounts would thus be offset by the interest paid on the money borrowed to create them, leaving the system right where it started.

Many would object that requiring families to save a portion of each year's income growth would be an infringement of individual liberty. Yet it is the very absence of such a requirement that currently prevents most American families from saving as much as they wish to. Just as nations find it advantageous to restrict their options by signing arms reduction treaties, families may have a similar interest in limiting their freedom to engage in bidding wars for houses in top school districts.

It is clear, in any event, that the failure to save entails risks of its own to freedom. America's rapidly rising indebtedness to foreigners now threatens the economic prosperity on which so many of our cherished liberties depend.

New York Times, March 17, 2005

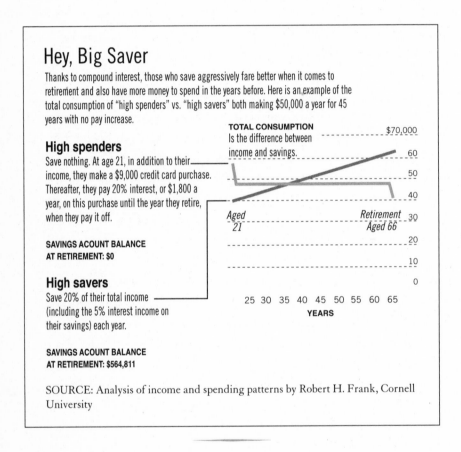

Hey, Big Saver

Thanks to compound interest, those who save aggressively fare better when it comes to retirement and also have more money to spend in the years before. Here is an example of the total consumption of "high spenders" vs. "high savers" both making $50,000 a year for 45 years with no pay increase.

High spenders
Save nothing. At age 21, in addition to their income, they make a $9,000 credit card purchase. Thereafter, they pay 20% interest, or $1,800 a year, on this purchase until the year they retire, when they pay it off.

SAVINGS ACOUNT BALANCE AT RETIREMENT: $0

High savers
Save 20% of their total income (including the 5% interest income on their savings) each year.

SAVINGS ACOUNT BALANCE AT RETIREMENT: $564,811

TOTAL CONSUMPTION
Is the difference between income and savings.

$70,000
60
50
40
30
20
10
0

Aged 21

Retirement Aged 66

25 30 35 40 45 50 55 60 65
YEARS

SOURCE: Analysis of income and spending patterns by Robert H. Frank, Cornell University

ALTHOUGH many thousands of people share responsibility for the financial crisis that began in 2008, some deserve special mention. First among them is former Republican senator Phil Gramm, a longtime champion of financial industry deregulation. In December 2000, Gramm inserted a last-minute provision into a Senate bill that prohibited regulation of the newly emerging financial derivative securities that played such a prominent role in the subsequent financial meltdown. And then there is former Fed chairman Alan Greenspan, who insisted that the financial industry could manage risk quite nicely without federal oversight. As Greenspan sheepishly admitted under questioning before the House Committee on Oversight and Government Reform on October 22, 2008, "Those of us who have looked to the self-interest of lending institutions to protect shareholders' equity, myself included, are in a state of shocked disbelief."

In the next selection, written during the fall of 2008, I suggest that Gramm and Greenspan were like many other traditional economists in their uncritical enthusiasm for Adam Smith's theory of the invisible hand—the idea that unfettered market forces will guide self-interested individuals to produce the greatest good for the greatest number. Had they taken a more active interest in the behavioral economics revolution, a lot of misery could have been averted.

51. Did Greed on Wall Street Cause the Financial Crisis?

Asset bubbles like the one that caused the current economic crisis have long plagued financial markets. But like hurricanes in the Gulf of Mexico, these disasters have been occurring with increasing frequency. If we want to prevent them, we must first understand their cause.

It isn't simply "Wall Street greed," which Senator John McCain has blamed for the crisis. Coming from McCain, a longtime champion of financial industry deregulation, it was a puzzling attribution, squarely at odds with the cherished belief of free market enthusiasts everywhere that unbridled pursuit of self-interest promotes the common good. As Adam Smith wrote in *Wealth of Nations*, "It is not from the benevolence of the butcher, the brewer, or the baker that we expect our dinner, but from their regard to their own interest."

Greed underlies every market outcome, good or bad. When important conditions are met, greed not only poses no threat to Smith's "invisible hand" of competition but is an essential part of it.

The forces that produced the current crisis actually reflect a powerful dynamic that afflicts all kinds of competitive endeavors, including sports. Consider a sprinter's decision about whether to take anabolic steroids. The sprinter's reward depends not on how fast he runs in absolute terms, but on how his times compare with those of others. Imagine a new drug that enhances performance by three-tenths of a second in the hundred-meter dash. Almost impossible to detect, it also entails a small risk of serious health problems. The sums at stake ensure that many competitors will take the drug, making it all but impossible for a drug-free competitor to win. The net effect is increased health risks for all athletes, with no real gain for society.

This particular type of market failure occurs when two conditions are met. First, people confront a gamble that offers a highly probable small gain with only a very small chance of a significant loss. Second, the rewards received by market participants depend strongly on relative performance.

These conditions have caused the invisible hand to break down in multiple domains. In unregulated housing markets, for example, there are invariably too many dwellings built on flood plains and in earthquake zones. Similarly, in unregulated labor markets, workers typically face excessive health and safety risks.

It is no different in unregulated financial markets, where easy credit terms almost always produce an asset bubble. The problem occurs because, just as in sports, an investment fund's success depends less on its absolute rate of return than on how that rate compares with those of rivals.

If one fund posts higher earnings than others, money immediately flows into it. And because managers are paid in proportion to how much money a fund oversees, they want to post relatively high returns at every moment.

One way to bolster a fund's return is to invest in slightly riskier assets. (Such investments generally pay higher returns because risk-averse investors would otherwise be unwilling to hold them.) Once some fund managers started offering higher-paying mortgage-backed securities (before the current crisis developed), others felt growing pressure to follow suit, lest their customers desert them.

Warren E. Buffett warned about a similar phenomenon during the tech bubble. Buffett said he wouldn't invest in tech stocks because he didn't understand the business model. Investors knew him to be savvy, but the relatively poor performance of his Berkshire Hathaway fund during the tech stock run-up persuaded many to move their money elsewhere. Buffett had the personal and financial resources to weather that storm. But most money managers did not, and the tech bubble kept growing.

A similar dynamic precipitated the current problems. The new mortgage-backed securities were catnip for investors. Many money managers knew that these securities were risky. As long as housing prices kept rising, however, they also knew that portfolios with high concentrations of the riskier assets would post higher returns, enabling them to attract additional investors. More important, they assumed that if things went wrong, there would be safety in numbers.

Phil Gramm, the former senator from Texas, and other proponents of financial industry deregulation insisted that market forces would provide ample protection against excessive risk. Lenders obviously don't want to make loans that won't be repaid, and borrowers have clear incentives to shop for favorable terms. And because everyone agrees that financial markets are highly competitive, Gramm's invocation of the familiar invisible hand theory persuaded many other lawmakers.

The invisible hand breaks down, however, when rewards depend heavily on relative performance. A high proportion of investors are simply unable to stand idly by while others earn conspicuously higher returns. This fact of human nature makes the invisible hand an unreliable shield against excessive financial risk.

Where do we go from here?

Many people advocate greater transparency in the market for poorly understood derivative securities. More stringent disclosure rules would be good but would not prevent future crises, any more than disclosing the relevant health risks would prevent athletes from taking steroids.

The only effective remedy is to change people's incentives. In sports, that means drug rules backed by strict enforcement. In financial markets, asset bubbles cause real trouble when investors can borrow freely to expand their holdings. To prevent such bubbles, we must limit the amounts that people can invest with borrowed money.

New York Times, October 5, 2008

THROUGHOUT recorded history, human societies have attempted to limit the interest rate that lenders are permitted to charge. Viewed through the lens of traditional economic models, such restrictions have always been a mystery. If a lender is willing to make a loan available on certain terms and if a borrower willingly accepts those terms, how does the state make either party better off by prohibiting their transaction?

Research in behavioral economics suggests a plausible answer to this question. In the next selection, I explain why—notwithstanding the protests of uncritical proponents of invisible hand theory—many people are simply not very good at making decisions that involve delayed consequences.

52. Should Payday Lending Be Restricted?

When a lion achieves alpha male status, one of his first acts is to kill all unrelated cubs in the pride. Is that a bad thing?

As biologists have long realized, the question makes little sense. In the bitterly competitive environments in which lions evolved, the dominant male's behavior was favored by natural selection because it brought females into heat more quickly, thus accelerating the transmission of his genes into the next generation. His behavior appears brutal to human onlookers and surely makes life less palatable for lions as a group. In the Darwinian framework, however, it is a simple fact of existence, neither good nor bad. In any event, such judgments have little practical significance, since moral outrage alone cannot prevent a dominant lion from killing cubs.

In contrast, when humans prey on weaker members of the community, others are quick to condemn them. More important, such denunciations often matter. Because complex networks of voluntary association underlie almost every human transaction, the bad opinion of others can threaten the survival of even the most powerful individuals and organizations.

But the supply of moral outrage is limited. To maximize its usefulness, it must be employed sparingly. The essential first step is to identify those who are responsible for bad outcomes. This is often harder than it appears. Failure at this stage steers anger toward people or groups whose behavior is, like the alpha lion's, an unavoidable consequence of environmental forces. In such instances, moral outrage would be better directed at those who enact the rules under which ostensibly bad actors operate.

A case in point is the outrage currently directed at lenders who extend credit at extremely high rates of interest to economically disadvantaged groups. Among these lenders, so-called payday loan shops have come under particularly heavy fire.

This industry, which didn't exist in the early 1990s, now has approximately 10,000 retail outlets nationwide (more in some states than either McDonald's or Burger King). Industry revenue, less than $1 billion in 1998, reached $28 billion last year.

Concentrated in low-income neighborhoods, payday lenders typically offer short-duration loans of several hundred dollars secured only by a postdated personal check from the borrower. Fees on a two-week loan often exceed $20 per $100 borrowed, which translates into an annual interest rate of more than 500 percent.

Occasional borrowing on such terms can make sense because it sidesteps the cumbersome process of taking out a traditional bank loan. Many borrowers, however, get into financial trouble once they begin to roll over their payday loans. A recent report by the Center for Responsible Lending, for example, estimated that a typical payday borrower ends up paying back $793 for a $325 loan.

Payday lenders have been condemned as ruthless predators whose greed drives hapless borrowers into financial ruin. Without question, the proliferation of payday lending has harmed many families. And since lenders surely know that, the moral outrage directed at them is understandable.

It may even have some effect. Economic studies suggest, for example, that employees demand premium wages for performing tasks that are considered morally objectionable. Outrage directed at payday lenders thus raises their hiring costs, which may inhibit their growth. But given the appetite for easy credit, this inhibition will be modest at best.

Those concerned about the growing culture of consumer debt need to recognize that it stems less from the greed of lenders than from liberalized lending laws. Since biblical days, societies have imposed limits on the terms under which people can borrow money. A wave of deregulation in the financial industry, however, has eliminated many of those limits. Liberalizing credit access may have made many mutually beneficial transactions possible, but its adverse consequences were completely predictable.

The problem is that many people have difficulty weighing the trade-off between immediate benefits and future costs. When confronted with easy credit access, some inevitably borrow more than they can reasonably expect to repay. Once they get in over their heads, they borrow more, if the law permits. It was thus all but certain that millions of society's most economically vulnerable members would borrow themselves into bankruptcy if confronted with easy credit access. If we are unhappy about that, our only recourse is to change the rules.

Each society must decide whether the costs of easy credit outweigh the benefits. This entails trade-offs similar to those we confront when deciding whether to regulate drugs. For example, alcoholic beverages, like payday loans, inflict considerable harm on a small percentage of people, but prohibiting alcohol appears to create more serious problems than it solves. Prohibiting cocaine and heroin entails troubling side effects too. Even so, concern for those most vulnerable to these drugs has led most societies to prohibit them.

Evidence suggests that easy credit access is more like heroin and cocaine than alcohol. This evidence recently led Congress to cap the annual interest rate on payday loans to military personnel at 36 percent. In New York and ten other states, similar restrictions apply to loans to the general public, in each case making payday lending effectively illegal.

Those who feel that payday lending is a bad thing are inclined to vent their anger about the hardships it has created. But outrage directed at payday lenders cannot prevent those hardships, just as outrage directed at alpha male lions cannot prevent them from killing cubs. A more deserving target would be legislators who supported lax credit laws in exchange for campaign contributions from lenders—or, better still, those who have steadfastly resisted campaign finance reform.

New York Times, January 18, 2007

AS the subprime mortgage crisis unfolded in 2008, there was spirited debate about the extent to which government should help families struggling to meet their mortgage payments. While compassion for these families explained part of the desire to help them, there was also a colder economic logic at work: additional foreclosures would mean more houses being put up for sale, which would accelerate the downward spiral in house prices and exacerbate the financial crisis. Weighing against aid were concerns about moral hazard—the worry that if people expected government to rescue families that had borrowed beyond their means, we would see even higher levels of irresponsible borrowing in the future.

In the following selection, I acknowledge the legitimacy of both concerns but argue that the mortgage crisis had less to do with blameworthy behavior on the part of borrowers than with changes in the terms on which the financial system made credit available to them.

53. Should Those Who Borrowed Too Much Be Punished?

After more than a decade of steep growth, home prices peaked last year and have been falling rapidly. Over 9 million mortgages are "under water," meaning that borrowers owe more than the home is worth. As foreclosures mount, additional homes come on the market, intensifying downward pressure on prices.

Congress is debating loan guarantees that would help homeowners renegotiate mortgages in default. In his initial response to the proposed legislation, Senator John McCain argued that "it is not the duty of government to bail out and reward those who act irresponsibly, whether they are big banks or small borrowers."

Many share McCain's concern. But while Congress clearly should not rescue borrowers who lied about their income or tried to get rich by flipping condos, such borrowers were a minor factor in this crisis. Primary responsibility rests squarely on regulators who permitted the liberal credit terms that created the housing bubble.

Hints of how things began to go awry appeared in *The Two-Income Trap,* a 2003 book in which Elizabeth Warren and Amelia Warren Tyagi posed this intriguing question: Why could families easily meet their financial obligations in the 1950s and 1960s, when only one parent worked outside the home, yet have great difficulty today, when two-income families are the norm? The answer, they suggest, is that the second incomes fueled a bidding war for housing in better neighborhoods.

It's easy to see why. Even in the 1950s, one of the highest priorities of most parents was to send their children to the best possible schools. Because the labor market has grown more competitive, this goal now looms even larger. It is no surprise that two-income families would choose to spend much of their extra income on better education. And because the best schools are in the most expensive neighborhoods, the imperative was clear: to gain access to the best possible public school, you must purchase the most expensive house you can afford.

But what works for an individual family does not work for society as a whole. The problem is that a "good" school is a relative concept: it is one that is better than other schools in the same area. When we all bid for houses in better school districts, we merely bid up the prices of those houses.

In the 1950s, as now, families tried to buy houses in the best school districts they could afford. But strict credit limits held the bidding in check. Lenders typically required down payments of 20 percent or more and would not issue loans for more than three times a borrower's annual income.

In a well-intentioned but ultimately misguided move to help more families enter the housing market, borrowing restrictions were relaxed during the intervening decades. Down payment requirements fell steadily, and in recent years, many houses were bought with no money down. Adjustable rate mortgages and balloon payments further boosted families' ability to bid for housing.

The result was a painful dilemma for any family determined not to borrow beyond its means. No one would fault a middle-income family for aspiring to send its children to schools of at least average quality. (How could a family aspire to less?) But if a family stood by while others exploited more liberal credit terms, it would consign its children to below-average schools. Even financially conservative families might have reluctantly concluded that their best option was to borrow up.

Those who condemn them see a different picture. They see undisciplined families overcome by their lust for cathedral ceilings and granite countertops, families that need to be taught a lesson.

Yet millions of families got into financial trouble simply because they understood that life is graded on the curve. The best jobs go to graduates from the best colleges, and because only the best-prepared students are accepted to those colleges, it is quixotic to expect parents to bypass an opportunity to send their children to the best elementary and secondary schools they can. The financial deregulation that enabled them to bid ever larger amounts for houses in the best school districts essentially guaranteed a housing bubble that would leave millions of families dangerously overextended.

Congress should not bail out speculators and fraudulent borrowers. But neither should it be too quick to condemn families that borrowed what the lending system offered rather than send their children to inferior schools.

Washington Post, April 27, 2008

A FIRMLY held belief among traditional economists is that asset markets are efficient. The price of a company's stock actually reflects its true economic value, or so the argument goes. The strongest version of the so-called efficient markets hypothesis holds that all new information relevant to a company's current and future earnings is almost immediately reflected in the price of its stock. This hypothesis implies, for example, that if unexpected new information became available at 10:00 AM on a weekday that a company's current and future earnings would be twice what they had been expected to be, the price of that company's stock would double within minutes.

In a weaker version of the efficient markets hypothesis, many economists concede that waves of optimism or pessimism may affect stock prices for extended periods. But even this version of the hypothesis insists that there is no cash on the table available to individual investors. The hapless individual investor just can't catch a break, they say; we can't beat the market. For example, even though stocks may be generally underpriced during periods of pessimism, individual investors typically have no practical means of identifying when the eventual turnaround will occur.

In the next selection, written during the height of the tech stock bubble in the spring of 2000, I try to explain why economists find the efficient markets hypothesis so compelling.

54. Why Is Trying to Beat the Market a Fool's Errand?

The story is told of two economists on their way to lunch who spot what appears to be a $100 bill lying on the sidewalk. When the younger economist stoops to pick up the bill, his older colleague restrains him, saying, "That can't be a $100 bill."

"Why not?" asks the younger colleague.

"If it were," comes the reply, "someone would have picked it up by now."

The older economist might have been wrong about that particular bill, of course. Yet his admonition embodies an important truth that Americans seem increasingly determined to ignore, namely, that low-hanging fruit in public places gets picked very quickly. As in the past, the only way to make real money in the future will be through some combination of talent, thrift, hard work, and luck.

Tens of millions of Americans, however, now seem to believe they can get rich in a hurry by simply transferring their money from old-economy stocks, like General Motors or Procter & Gamble, into Oracle, Cisco Systems, and other high-tech stocks that have led the Nasdaq index.

So far that strategy has worked like a charm. Someone who invested $100,000 in the Nasdaq index in January 1992 is now holding shares that are worth more than $850,000, and that takes this week's ups and downs into account. Many bullish analysts insist that the ride is far from over, and no one can doubt that the new technologies have thus far generated only a tiny fraction of the gains in productivity they will ultimately produce. It may be no exaggeration, for example, to say that business-to-business e-commerce will reduce the operating costs of many companies by 30 percent or more.

The ultimate value of an e-commerce company, however, depends not on the gains made possible by its technology but on how much profit it generates.

As in the past, new technologies will continue to generate a burst of new profits for companies that are relatively quick to adopt them. But the historical pattern has been that competition will award the long-run savings from these technologies to consumers in the form of lower prices.

Thus dairy farmers who were quick to adopt bovine somato-tropin, the hormone that increases milk yields by as much as 20 percent, reaped a short-term windfall. But as use of the hormone spread, increased production pushed milk prices steadily downward, eroding profit margins.

A similar profit trajectory will characterize most Nasdaq purveyors of new technologies. Organizers of business-to-business e-commerce may indeed save manufacturers hundreds of billions of dollars. But because the new technology companies are no more insulated from competition than dairy farmers, most of those savings will take the form of lower product prices, not higher profits.

Armed with this simple insight, economists have long warned investors against betting their entire fortunes on new technology companies. Many sophisticated portfolio managers share these concerns.

The reality, however, is that investors who want to insulate themselves from risk have no safe haven in today's market.

The cautious investor's natural inclination is to focus on old-economy stocks that are not yet selling for astronomical multiples of their annual earnings. Yet investing in those companies entails another form of risk. If millions of Americans continue putting their money behind high-tech companies each month, someone who fails to buy Nasdaq stocks will miss out on the greatest financial bonanza in generations.

Thus far the latter risk is the one people seem intent on avoiding. The small handful of investment firms whose cautious managers built portfolios that were light on high-tech stocks in recent years have seen their clients depart in droves. For such firms, to continue advising against high-tech stocks is to risk extinction. Earlier this week, the Nasdaq index plunged almost 9.3 percent from its peak of more than 5,000, set just last Friday. At the same time, the old-economy stocks of the Dow Jones industrials staged a modest rebound.

Is this the beginning of a major realignment, notwithstanding the index's gains yesterday? Someone who knew the answer to that question would not have to work for a living.

But the likely outcome is that the pattern of recent years will continue a while longer. After all, the Nasdaq has swooned many times during its protracted run-up, and each time investors have rushed in to buy tech stocks at the new "bargain" prices, as they seem to have done again yesterday.

If the Nasdaq's upward spiral resumes, more investors will feel compelled to jump on board. In such an environment, the only thing certain is that a spectacular downturn lies out there somewhere.

New York Times, March 17, 2000

EVEN when the tech stock bubble of the 1990s was in full swing, many experienced Wall Street observers cautioned that stocks were trading at unsustainably high prices. Similar warnings were heard in the months before the financial meltdown of 2008. But the fact that these warnings proved well founded doesn't mean it was a mistake to buy or hold stocks. Buying an overpriced stock today can make perfect sense if you think you'll be able to sell it at an even higher price before the downturn comes. In this chapter's final selection, written during the fall of 1999, I describe the obsessive attention characteristic of amateur investors following the latest market news.

55. Can Government Financial Data Help You Get Rich?

As recently as the 1980s, hardly anyone outside the financial industry took an interest in forecasting stock prices. An exception was a colleague of mine, a professor who actively managed his own portfolio long before the advent of Internet trading. His crowning achievement was predicting the October 1987 crash with greater accuracy than most experts. In the weeks following the crash, many stepped forward claiming to have seen it coming, but almost alone among them, my colleague had taken nearly all of his money out of the market just weeks before it happened. In the risk-averse world of tenured academics, this gutsy move earned him instant superstar status.

These days, of course, one seldom meets anyone who is *not* an expert stock picker. A natural outgrowth of this phenomenon has recently begun to take form: this nation of stock pickers is rapidly turning into a nation of economic forecasters.

The mainstream media's coverage of hard economic data used to be perfunctory: a spot of news about the direction of interest rates or a calculation of how the dollar was holding up against the yen. Now these reports have grown bewilderingly detailed and complex. One recent morning, a cable-network newsreader reported with a straight face that although the monthly trade deficit had shown a sharp decline in the quarter just ended, the movement should not be interpreted as a positive indicator because export figures contained a large commercial aircraft shipment that markets had known about for months in advance. Another correspondent advised viewers that the rise in the wholesale price index should be discounted heavily, because much of it was attributable to movements in traditionally volatile energy components of the index.

Every day, some government agency reports at least one major figure, and the financial news channels cover it with the pageantry and suspense of the Academy Awards nominations. A couple of weeks ago, the menu for the daily feast went like this: Monday was business inventories, Tuesday was a double dose of industrial production and capacity utilization, Wednesday we got the Consumer Price Index, housing starts, and building permits, and Thursday was international trade. Friday, we were permitted to rest.

I'm a university economist and the author of several books about economics, and even I had to ask, Who cares? Aside from people whose work depends on these figures, who would be interested in them? And what in the world can individual investors possibly learn from this endless torrent of information? When we find out that sales of existing homes in the Southwest were expected to rise 0.3 percent in September but actually rose only 0.25 percent, should we shift our portfolio to firms in the Pacific Northwest? Or divest our portfolios of stock in roofing nail suppliers?

Whatever we decide to do, it's a sure bet that the market has already beaten us to it. Economists disagree about many things, but one belief we share is that investors can almost never make financial headway by trading on the basis of numbers they hear about through the media.

Yet if anything, the number of financial news outlets has continued to proliferate in recent months. Countless new websites and cable channels and newsletters and email services urge their services upon us. Indeed, the reporting of financial trivia now threatens to drown out all other news. This information does serve an important function, just not the one it claims to serve.

Old-style Wall Street cognoscenti have generally stuck to the view that the current boom must come to an end. We may wake up one morning to find all those paper billions up in smoke. But as the market has continued its ascent, swelling our faith in ourselves as master investors, fatalism has been tempered by the idea that a crash need not take down everyone. In a world in which investors make millions from trading stock in companies that may never earn a dime, official economic data provide a reassuring kind of white noise. They won't help the citizen investor predict whether Amazon stock is a good buy, but they're pure and direct and unimpeachable: This is your government talking, this is the state of your country. More than that, the numbers make this tantalizing promise: if we just keep watching them, maybe we'll spot the inevitable downturn in time to bail out.

But if and when the crash does come, the number crunchers who manage to get out in time will confront a second challenge—deciding when to get back in. And here the experience of my colleague who sold out just before the 1987 crash sounds a cautionary note. "I thought prices would continue to decline for at least the next year," he once told me with chagrin, "so I wasn't eager to get back in the market right away." But as often happens, prices began to recover almost immediately after the October downturn, and by the time my colleague finally got back into the market in mid-1988, prices were higher than when he'd sold. He has no illusions that he'd have done any better if only that critical capacity utilization report had been blasted over the airwaves back then.

New York Times Magazine, November 28, 1999

12

The Economics of Information

The models in most standard economics textbooks assume that market participants are perfectly informed about all relevant opportunities and constraints they face, so no one knows something important that others don't. Needless to say, this assumption is not intended to describe any actual market participant. There is just too much information out there for anyone to be able to process and make use of more than a minuscule fraction of it.

Still, the assumption of perfect information is a reasonable abstraction much of the time. Consider, for example, that most students who attend college do so within a year or two of graduating from high school. Why don't more of them wait until they're in their forties or fifties? An economist armed with the perfect information model would say it's because the relevant costs and benefits make early education compellingly more advantageous. The logic goes something like this: wage rates rise with age and experience, which means that the earnings that must be forgone to attend college are lowest right out of high school. In addition, the sooner you get a degree, the more years you get to enjoy the higher earnings that generally accompany additional education.

Noneconomists often dismiss this explanation on the grounds that they've never met anyone who actually engaged in such deliberations before deciding when to start college. But an economic model can be useful even if it doesn't literally describe the thought processes that unfold inside the decision maker's head. Most students start college shortly after finishing high school simply because that's long been the custom. But how did it come to be the custom? For argument's sake, suppose everyone chose the length of the interval between high school and college at random. Because large groups of people make this decision each year, relevant experience would accumulate about which length of interval seems to work best. A collective wisdom would eventually emerge that shorter intervals between high school and college yield more favorable outcomes. A similar learning-by-doing interpretation would apply to decisions that each individual confronts repeatedly.

For these types of decisions, the standard economic model can be viewed as saying that people behave *as if* they were fully rational and in possession of all relevant information. Other decisions, however, aren't like that at all. One-shot decisions like which doctor to see, which candidate to vote for, or which used car to buy are necessarily made with imperfect and incomplete information.

Not having full information is not always the same thing as being completely in the dark. As former Defense secretary, Donald Rumsfeld once remarked during a news conference, "There are known knowns. There are things we know that we know. There are known unknowns. That is to say, there are things that we now know we don't know. But there are also unknown unknowns. There are things we do not know we don't know."

Decision makers can employ even fragmentary information to construct reasonable estimates of the things they know they don't know. The selected columns included in this chapter deal with situations in which people know they don't have specific information that would be relevant for the decisions they face. In the first selection, written during the 2008 presidential primaries, I consider the question of what we can infer when candidates conceal potentially relevant information about their health or financial status.

56. Are There Any Real Secrets?

Ordinary citizens cherish the right to shield their personal financial and medical records from public view. Presidential candidates, by contrast, are expected to disclose such information in fine-grained detail. It's a reasonable expectation because candidates' financial and health records are often relevant to voters' decisions.

Yet because such information is often intensely personal, many candidates are reluctant to make it public. In the current election cycle, for example, Senator Hillary Rodham Clinton released her family's recent tax returns only after enduring protracted criticism for failing to do so.

Senator John McCain, for his part, has not yet released his recent tax returns or medical records, although he has promised to make them available soon.

Such reluctance flies in the face of an important principle from the economic theory that governs communication between potential adversaries. Known as the full disclosure principle, it holds that rivals should find it advantageous to disclose all possible information about themselves that others might consider relevant, even when the information is unflattering.

The principle is neatly illustrated by the behavior of male frogs competing for the same mate. In many species, a smaller animal generally defers to a larger, more powerful opponent. But frogs are nocturnal and often can't determine the size of rivals visually. Instead, they croak. The frog with the higher-pitched croak, which is almost always smaller, defers to the one with the lower pitch.

But why would any high-pitched frog bother to croak in the first place, thereby revealing how small it is? Why not just remain silent?

Economists have an answer: A frog that stays silent would be assumed to be even less formidable than it really is. To see why, imagine that all high-pitched frogs remain quiet. One is bigger than all others, yet its silence suggests that it is of average size for its group. This frog does better to croak, so it does. And so does the next biggest frog, and on and on, until only the smallest frog is left.

The full disclosure principle thus suggests why individuals sometimes divulge unflattering information about themselves. Their silence might encourage observers to draw even less flattering inferences. Yet, as recent experience involving candidates' tax returns and medical records demonstrates, the prediction that people will voluntarily disclose such information is clearly wide of the mark.

Why? So far at least, the answer doesn't seem to be that the returns were withheld because they contained the least flattering information possible.

As commentators were quick to point out, the Clinton tax returns revealed that the couple has earned an enormous sum—$109 million—since leaving the White House. But that is certainly not as unflattering as a disclosure could be.

The tax returns of Senator Barack Obama, who took the lead in the latest round of financial disclosure, showed a similar, if less spectacular, spike in recent income. There were no big surprises, though some commentators complained that the Obamas had donated a relatively small percentage of their income to charity.

If Senator McCain eventually releases his tax returns and post-2000 medical records, they too will be scrutinized and may well be similarly devoid of big surprises. In fact, it seems reasonable to assume that they will fall far short of the most negative information people might imagine.

And yet Clinton and McCain seemed willing to endure extensive criticism for their failure to disclose personal information more promptly, apparently preferring to let voters imagine the worst.

A possible reason for the breakdown of the full disclosure principle is evident in more mundane cases. Although it predicts that someone would never say "You can't come over now because my apartment's such a mess" (because such statements should provoke the conclusion that the apartment was as messy as an apartment could be), people actually make such statements about their apartments all the time.

The disconnect stems from the difference between how we are affected by logical inference on the one hand and actual experience on the other. It is one thing to conclude logically that someone's apartment must be messy. It is quite another to confront the stench of rotting garbage in the kitchen. In a case like this, it's probably better to let your friends imagine what they will.

Similar considerations may inhibit disclosure by politicians. Sometimes it may seem best to leave unpleasant details to the conjecture of others.

Still, the full disclosure principle provides some useful insight into candidates' behavior, to a point. It may help to explain why David A. Paterson, who became governor of New York in the wake of Eliot Spitzer's resignation, was so quick to disclose unflattering personal information that went beyond what many of his constituents seemed eager to learn. But the principle's simple logic does not explain why so many politicians are so reluctant to disclose seemingly basic personal financial and medical information.

The plain fact is that it is much harder for journalists to write about imaginary problems, even big ones, that might be lurking in unreleased tax returns and medical records, than to write about actual problems, even small ones, that turn up in the records themselves.

Voluntary disclosure has clear limits. And because voters have legitimate reasons for wanting to be well informed about the health and finances of candidates for high office, disclosure requirements need to be strict. On these subjects, politicians all too often remain silent.

New York Times, April 13, 2008

IN recent years, behavioral economists have been joining forces with neuroscientists in an attempt to discover how the human brain processes information relevant for economic decisions. In 2005 I had the pleasure of collaborating with two distinguished New York University neuroscientists on a study of how preconceptions about others affect how we process relevant information about them. I wrote the next selection in response to an invitation from the editors of *Worth* magazine to summarize the findings of our study for their readers.

57. Does Prejudice Interfere with Normal Learning?

An experimenter hands you $100, which you can keep. But if you return it, she will give $300 to a stranger, who can either keep it all or keep only half and give you the remaining $150.

Returning the $100 is a gamble. If the stranger shares, you get $50 more than if you had kept it. But if he doesn't share, you get nothing. What would you do?

This experiment is called the "trust game." In a recent study, NYU neuroscientists Elizabeth Phelps, Mauricio Delgado, and I employed it to discover how information about potential partners affects how people evaluate situations involving trust.

We told participants they would play the game with three fictional partners described as having either praiseworthy, neutral, or suspect moral character. In attempting to make our descriptions sufficiently vivid to trigger emotions implicated in trust decisions, we concluded each character's portrait with an ostensible newspaper account of a recent life experience. For example, this mock article from the *Iowa Press Citizen* followed the good character's description:

— LOCAL HERO —

Former Iowa City resident Christopher Thompson was at the Station Concert Club in West Warwick, Rhode Island, when fire broke out on the evening of February 20, killing 98 people. While visiting relatives in Providence, he had gone to the club with Tom Battle, a high school classmate, and Battle's wife, Susan.

Thompson was seated at a table near an exit when the fire started. The Battles, however, were standing among scores of other spectators crowded near the stage, where Great White, a heavy metal band, had just begun its first set.

After leading several others out of the club to safety, Thompson went back inside in an attempt to locate the Battles. Tom Battle was nowhere in sight, but Thompson quickly spotted Susan Battle lying unconscious on the floor. He managed to drag her to safety moments before the building collapsed in flames. In the process, he suffered third-degree burns on his neck, left arm, and hand.

Thompson, 26, was released from a Providence hospital on February 27.

The bad character's article reported his recent arrest for selling tiles from the failed space shuttle Columbia on eBay. The neutral character's article reported his arrival moments too late for a flight that crashed shortly after takeoff.

Participants were warned that their partners' computer-generated responses might not match their portrayals. In fact, all were programmed to share half the time.

Despite this warning, participants initially transferred money much more often to good partners than to others. But having completed multiple trials with each type, participants reported correctly that the different types were sharing at about the same rate. *Strikingly, however, they continued to be more trusting with good partners.*

As they were informed whether their partners had shared, functional magnetic resonance imaging of participants' brains recorded activation in the caudate nucleus, a region linked to reward processing during trial and error learning. But we observed the traditional response patterns only during interactions with neutral partners. Activation was either weak or absent during other interactions. Prior impressions of good and bad partners thus appeared to disrupt normal learning mechanisms.

Although folk wisdom stresses the durability of first impressions, economic models predict that opinions will be updated on receipt of relevant new information about exchange partners. Our study supports the folk wisdom position. Once primed with a biased portrait, our basic learning mechanisms don't function as economists envision.

That we often take appearances at face value might tempt some businesses to portray themselves as trustworthy, the better to exploit their customers. But this strategy entails risk. If self-proclaimed trustworthiness has no factual basis, its inevitable unmasking will command more attention than the original portrayal. The resulting negative impressions will be as persistent as the initial positive ones.

Once customers feel burned, they often are willing to incur considerable costs to punish the offender. This was shown by the neuroscientist Dominique de Quervain and several colleagues, whose trust game allowed the additional option of paying for the right to impose financial penalties on partners who hadn't shared. Many seized this opportunity. Brain scans suggest they experienced their revenge as pleasurable.

Bottom line: the durability of reputation is a double-edged sword. The good opinion of others is a valuable asset that, once lost, is difficult to recover. Perhaps the surest path to the advantages of appearing trustworthy is actually to be trustworthy.

Worth, April 2006

MANY hiring decisions are necessarily made with fragmentary information. Employers are often uncertain about what skills a new position will demand. But even when it's a long-standing position whose requirements they know well, they are unlikely to have reliable information about the extent to which a given applicant possesses the relevant skills. Résumés and recommendations often don't reveal much about actual performance. Job applicants, for their part, typically have an imperfect notion of what the positions they seek will require of them.

Even more troubling is the possibility that preconceptions about specific groups may distort perceptions in ways that make it unlikely to achieve the best matchup between applicants and positions. A long-standing argument by traditional economists is that competition helps limit the effects of discrimination by employers on the basis of race and sex. In the following selection, written just after the 2008 election, I describe this argument and consider the extent to which it applies in two specific domains, presidential politics and professional sports.

58. Does Competition Eliminate Job Discrimination?

While campaigning in western Pennsylvania last month, Barack Obama was asked whether racial bias might hurt his campaign. "What I've found is that people here, they don't care what color you are," Obama told a Pittsburgh television reporter. "What they're trying to figure out is, who can deliver? It's just like the Pittsburgh Steelers. They don't care what color you are, they want to make sure you can make the plays."

Obama's comments didn't cite Milton Friedman directly, but they may be read as an implicit endorsement of the late Nobel laureate's claim that competitive markets are the surest way to eliminate job discrimination. Friedman, the conservative thinker who taught at the University of Chicago years before Obama's arrival there, advanced this position forcefully in his 1962 book, *Capitalism and Freedom.*

The Friedman argument rests on the observation that when business owners don't hire the most qualified candidate, they pay a price.

Some owners might be happy to discriminate if they could do so without penalty, Friedman conceded. But discrimination in a free market is always costly, he said. If owners hire a white candidate who is less able than a black candidate they could have hired, profits suffer. Friedman argued that most owners would conclude that discrimination simply isn't worth it. (Friedman, of course, had no illusions that competition would eliminate the disadvantages that stem from growing up poor or attending substandard schools.)

The notion that employer discrimination will be eliminated by competition is appealing, but it's not consistent with field experiments suggesting that such bias in labor markets remains widespread. In a 2004 paper published in the *American Economic Review*, for example, Marianne Bertrand and Sendhil Mullainathan, professors of economics at the University of Chicago and Harvard, respectively, found that applicants named Lakisha or Jamal were less likely to be considered for jobs, even when they had qualifications on paper that were similar to those of applicants named Emily or Greg. In response to job advertisements in Boston and Chicago newspapers, the economists submitted fictitious résumés and cover letters under the two sets of names. Candidates with the Anglo names, they reported, were significantly more likely to be invited for interviews.

Many economists concede the validity of Milton Friedman's argument when all participants in a labor market are well-informed, particularly employers, who would need precise measures of applicants' abilities to estimate how costly discrimination would be. In reality, though, hiring decisions are often made under time pressure with imperfect information about candidates. In a 2005 paper jointly written with Dolly Chugh, a New York University management professor, Bertrand and Mullainathan argued that under these circumstances, labor market discrimination may persist, albeit outside the conscious awareness of those who make hiring decisions.

Friedman's argument is clearly most persuasive when labor market conditions come closest to the full-information competitive ideal described in textbooks. So Obama's invocation of the Pittsburgh

Steelers was well chosen for the point he was making. Professional sports markets may not match the textbook ideal, but they are at least as competitive as other labor markets and have no shortage of data on candidates.

For example, teams hire high-priced scouts who spend thousands of hours gathering detailed data about individual prospects before deciding whom to draft or hire as free agents. Won-lost records provide a conspicuous measure of success. And while corporations often retain employees who are well past their productive prime, professional athletes who have lost a step are usually cut promptly. In short, professional sports provides as forceful an example as we are likely to find of a market in which the color of a person's skin is irrelevant.

By contrast, the job market for presidents—the election campaign, culminating in the actual vote on Election Day—may be the best method we've come up with for choosing a national leader, but as I'll explain, it bears little resemblance to the textbook ideal of a perfectly competitive job market.

In 2008, however, an unusual confluence of circumstances made the resemblance much closer than usual. With the economy in the midst of its most serious downward spiral since the Great Depression, voters were forcefully reminded that the quality of the person they elected could have enormous implications for their own well-being. The campaign also began earlier and confronted voters with a tremendous amount of information, on the Internet as well as through traditional media, about the candidates' positions and achievements.

In typical campaigns, candidates stick to carefully prepared scripts that many voters find difficult to distinguish. But this year's volatile climate forced candidates to react to events on the fly, often in full public view. And in addition to whatever impressions they were forming on their own, many voters were undoubtedly influenced by trusted figures like Warren E. Buffett, Paul A. Volcker, and Colin L. Powell, who were telling them that Obama was the better choice.

All told, the 2008 campaign made it hard to deny the importance of choosing a candidate who could "make the plays." Under these circumstances, even some strongly prejudiced voters might have found the price of indulging their bias too steep. If the stakes had been lower, race might well have been a bigger issue. Even so, Obama's election could mean that race will henceforth always matter less, as the world of professional sports suggests.

There were no black major league baseball players before Branch Rickey, the Brooklyn Dodgers team president, added Jackie Robinson to his roster in 1947. During Robinson's ten-year career with the team, he was voted to the National League All-Star team six times, and the Dodgers went to the World Series six times. In retirement, he was elected to Baseball's Hall of Fame on the first ballot. Shortly after Robinson's arrival in the major leagues, it became clear to all that failure to field the best possible team, irrespective of color, was a sure recipe for failure.

As events unfold, it will be interesting to see whether Obama changes voting practices as much as Robinson changed hiring practices in baseball.

New York Times, November 16, 2008

Index

Aaron Faber Gallery, 15
Affluent Society, The (Galbraith), 76, 77
Akerlof, George A., 76
Alesina, Alberto, 29, 167
Alpha magazine, 148
Altman, Robert, 141, 191
America Online. *See* AOL-TimeWarner merger
American Economic Review, 224
American Economics Association, 88
Ames, Ruth, 38
Antigovernment crusaders, 16–19
Antipoverty policies, 18
AOL-TimeWarner merger, 159–162
Archer, Bill, 65
AT&T, 146, 147
Aumann, Robert J., 73, 74

Balet, Greg, 86
Bankruptcy, 94, 107, 204
    income inequality and, 167, 177
    luxury spending and, 181, 191
Barry, Dave, 140
Battle, Susan and Tom, 221
Baylor Regional Medical Center, 95–96
Becker, Gary S., 129
Behavioral economics, 4, 5–6, 79, 220–222

Bentham, Jeremy, 53
Berkshire Hathaway fund, 201
Bertrand, Marianne, 224
Bipartisan Reform Act of 2002, 49, 50
Bloomberg, Michael R., 113, 114, 115
Boorstin, Daniel, 91–92
Bovine somatotropin, 210
Bradley, Bill, 108
Bradsher, Keith, 120, 137, 141
Brookings Institution, 26
Brooklyn Dodgers, 226
Brooks, David H., 15
Bruner, Jerome, 90
Budget deficits, Federal, 11–13, 30–32, 33, 166
Buffett, Warren E., 27, 201, 225
Bush, George W. and his administration, 23, 24, 42, 129
    budget deficits of, 30–31, 166
    health care and, 95–96, 98, 105–106
    Social Security and, 194, 197
    tax cuts of, 10–13, 20–22, 30–31, 33–34, 44, 98, 106
Business Week, 143, 165

California Air Resources Board, 101
Campaigns, political, 48–51
    See also Presidential candidates

Capitalism and Freedom (Friedman), 47, 223

Carbon dioxide emissions, 101, 103, 113

Cargo inspections, 12–13, 22, 34, 77, 151

Carter, Jimmy, 128

Center for Responsible Lending, 204

Center on Budget and Policy Priorities, 23

Cheney, Dick, 129

Chugh, Dolly, 224

Civil Aeronautics Board (CAB), 118, 119–120

Class warfare, 169–172

Clinton administration, 105, 106, 107, 108

Clinton, Hillary Rodham, 4, 133, 135, 217, 218

Cloning Technologies, 145–147

Colbert, Stephen, 98

Columbia Business School, 150

Command-and-control regulations, 125–126

Commuters, 186–188

Competition, 154–155, 199
    in animal kingdom, 202–203, 205, 217–218
    internet businesses and, 161–162
    and job discrimination, 222–226

Compound interest, 194–199

Congestion Pricing, 113–116

Consumption, 182–183
    taxes, 31–33, 82, 184–186, 190–191
    theories regarding, 70–71, 77–78
    See also Spending

Context, 2–3, 4, 11, 72, 174–177, 183, 184

Cook, Philip, 144

Cornell University, Survey Research Institute, 24, 25 (table)

Corporations, 50, 94, 145

Cost-benefit theories, 6–7, 137–138
    and economic education, 86, 87–89
    of gasoline, 137–138
    and health care, 96–97
    See also Pricing

Credit access
    Mortgage crisis and, 205–208
    Payday lending and, 202–205

Credit card debts, 181, 195–196

Darwinian framework, 202–203

DavosNewbies.com, 86

Death taxes. *See* Estate taxes

Debts, 181, 195–196
    See also Federal budget deficits

Delgado, Mauricio, 220

Desire, human, 55–57

Disclosure principle, 217–219

Domenici, Pete V., 12, 33

Duesenberry, James S., 70–73, 193

Dulski, Jennifer, 90, 91

Dunand, Jean, 15

Earned income tax credit, 18–19, 65, 81–82

eBay, 157–158

"Economic naturalist" assignment, 85–86, 89–90, 91

Economic Naturalist, The (Frank), 8, 89

"Economic Possibilities for Our Grandchildren" (Keynes), 55

Economics education
    as ineffective, 84–87
    introduced, 83–84
    and Opportunity Cost Concept, 87–89
    of pricing, 111–112
    writing to aid in, 89–92

Economics of information
    behavioral economics and, 220–222
    disclosure principle and, 217–219

hiring decisions and, 222–223
introduced, 215–217
Education, 143–144, 152–156
    information model and, 215–216
    quality schools for, 75, 170–171,
        196, 206–208
    See also Economics education
Edwards, Elizabeth, 30
Edwards, John, 27
Efficiency, 5–6, 131, 133–136,
    208–211
Emanuel, Ezekiel, 99
Emissions, 101, 103, 113, 125–126
Employer discrimination, 222–226
Energy policies, 19, 30, 125–127, 131
Environmental issues, 1–2, 60,
        126–127
    gasoline and, 127–133
    global warming and, 121, 130
    of greenhouse gases, 102, 103, 125
    negative externalities and,
        125–126, 136
    and SUVs, 121, 123
    See also Emissions; Pollution
Equity, 5–6, 150–151
Equity and Efficiency (Okun), 5
Estate taxes, 22–27, 25 (table)
Ethics, 39–42, 42–44
Expenses. *See* Spending
Externalities, negative, 125–126, 136

Faber, Edward, 15
Fair Labor Standards Act, 75–76
Far Side (Larson), 155
Federal Aviation Administration,
    118, 119
Federal budget deficits, 11–13,
    30–32, 33, 166
Federal Election Campaign Act,
    49
Federal Government. *See*
    Government
Ferraro, Paul J., 88, 89
Fidler, Lewis A., 114

Financial
    aid, 152–155
    distress, 168–172, 177–178, 186
    records of presidential candidates,
        217–219
    See also Money
First Amendment, 49–50, 51
Fleischer, Ari, 186–188
Ford, William Clay Jr., 121, 123
Foreclosures. *See* Mortgage crisis
Foreign policies, fuel, 136–139
Frank, Robert H., 8, 59, 67, 99
    Civil Aeronautics Board and, 118
    eBay shares and, 157–159
    and France, 37–38, 56–57
    and newspaper columns, 4–5
    Peace Corps training of, 85, 177
Free speech. *See* First Amendment
Friedman, Benjamin, 60, 64
Friedman, Milton, 47, 71–72, 77, 78
    competitive markets and, 223–224
    economic theories of, 80–82
Frisch, Ragnar, 79
Fuchs, Victor, 99
Fuel subsidies, 136–139
    See also Gasoline
Full disclosure principles, 217–219
Funt, Allen, 140

Galbraith, John Kenneth, 6, 76–79
Gasoline, 142
    costs of, 137–138
    taxes on, 127–133, 134–136
Gates, Bill, 171
General Electric, 159–160
Gilovich, Tom, 69, 73
Global warming, 121, 130
Gore, Al, 108, 147, 169
Government, 16–19, 168
    deregulation of, 198–199, 204
    Good, 50, 50–51
    state versus federal, 101–104
    See also Federal budget deficits
Gramm, Phil, 198–199, 201

Great Crash of 1929, The (Galbraith), 76
Great Depression, The, 76, 197, 225
Greenhouse gases, 102, 103, 125
Greenspan, Alan, 30–31, 199
Gross Domestic Product (GDP), 61–64
Growth, Economic, 58, 60, 61–64, 182

Habtegiris, Tirhas, 95–97
Happiness, 53–56, 182–183
    See also Money and happiness
Harry Potter (Rowling), 155, 156, 157
Health care, 12, 18, 93–94, 177, 217
    boutique, 104–106
    insurance and, 98–101, 106–109
    state versus federal, 101–104
    of terminally ill patients, 95–97
    traffic congestion and, 186–188
    universal, 27–28, 30, 33, 94
    See also Single payer health care system
Hedge fund managers, 148–151
Herd instincts, 139–142
Hertz, Thomas, 167
High and Mighty (Bradsher), 120, 140
Hirschman, Albert O., 46
Home foreclosures, 205–208
Hornstein, Harvey, 35
House Ways and Means Committee, 65

Incentives, 184–185, 190, 202
Income. *See* Money
Income inequality, 163–164, 197
    class warfare and, 168–172
    comparison envy and, 173–178
    luxury spending and, 179–186
    reasons for, 164–168
    and traffic congestion, 186–188

Income taxes. *See* Tax cuts; Taxes
Inconspicuous consumption, 182–183
Inefficiency, 78–79, 131, 133–136
Inflation, 61–63
Information. *See* Economics of information
Insurance companies, 98–101, 106–109
Interest, 194–199, 202
Internet access. *See* AOL-TimeWarner merger
Intuit, 144
Investments, 195, 200–202
    See also Stock Market
Invisible hand theories, 74–76, 136, 199
    breaking down of, 201
    effects of, 133–134, 183
Iowa Press Citizen, 220–221

Job creation, 19, 20–22
Job discrimination, 222–226
John S. and James L. Knight Foundation, 90
J.P. Morgan, 153

Kahn, Alfred E., 114, 118
Kahneman, Daniel, 73
Keillor, Garrison, 153
Kennedy, John F., 5, 47
Keynes, John Maynard, 54–56, 57, 143
Kiplinger, 144
Knobel, Lance, 86

La Guardia Airport, 118–120
Landsburg, Steven E., 95, 96–97
Larson, Gary, 155
Laws, 3–4, 48–51
Lawyers, 26, 151
Layard, Richard, 11
Leach, Robin, 168–169
Learning. *See* Education
Lerner, Abba, 135

Lifestyles of the Rich and Famous, 168–169

Limbaugh, Rush, 10, 23, 30

Living standards, 177, 181–182

Loans, 3–4, 13, 21, 202–205
  See also Mortgage crisis

Logic of Collective Action, The (Olson), 45

Low-income populace. *See* Poor populace

Luxury Fever (Frank), 178

Luxury spending, 77, 78, 179–186, 188–191
  See also Spending

MacCulloch, Robert, 168

Mankiw, N. Gregory, 129

Marginal cost, 112–113, 132

Markets, efficient, 208–211

Markets, winner-take-all, 143–147

Marwell, Gerald, 38

Massachusetts Institute of Technology, 154

McCain, John, 199, 206
  disclosure principle and, 217, 218
  tax cuts and, 20, 133, 135

McCain-Feingold law, 49, 50, 51

Mencken, H. L., 176

Mergers, 151

Micromotives and Macrobehavior (Schelling), 73

Middle class
  financial distress of, 168–172, 177–178, 186
  spending of, 65–66
  taxes of, 28, 32

Minimum wages, 18–19

Modern game theory, 78

Mondell, Kevin and Danya, 16

Money, 27, 48–51, 72, 217–219
  distribution from rich to poor, 16–19, 27–30
  federal budget deficits and, 11–13, 30–32, 33, 166

and inflation, 61–63
  and interest, 194–199, 202
  investments, 195, 200–202
  markets, 143–147, 208–211
  minimum wage and, 18–19
  See also Bankruptcy; Income inequality; Savings; Spending; Stock Market

Money and happiness
  correlated with well-being, 57–60, 62–63, 67
  human desire and, 54–57
  introduced, 53–55

Moral Consequences of Economic Growth (Friedman), 60

Mortgage crisis, 205–208

Mullainathan, Sendhil, 224

Nasdaq index, 209, 210–211

National debt. *See* Federal budget deficits

National Institutes of Health, 99

National security, 12–13

Negative externalities, 125–126, 136

Negative income tax, 80–82

Neumark, Dave, 176

Neuroscientists, 220, 221–222

New Yorker, 36

New York Mets, 116–117

New York State Public Service Commission, 114–115

New York Times, 5, 14, 67, 70, 132, 137, 141, 159, 172, 188, 211

Nobel Peace Prize, 73, 74, 76–79

Norquist, Grover, 129

Nunn, Sam, 12, 33

Obama, Barack, 5, 47, 218
  presidential campaign of, 45, 48, 50–51
  racial bias and, 223, 224–225, 226

Oil, 136–139
  See also Gasoline

Olson, Mancur, 45

Oogles-n-Googles company, 16
Opportunity Cost Concept, 87–89
"Optimistic Parents" (Larson),
    155–156
Organization for Economic
    Co-operation, 29
Organization of the Petroleum
    Exporting Countries (OPEC),
    130–131
Osborne, Tom, 14

Pataki, George E., 101
Paterson, David A., 219
Payday lending, 202–205
Phelps, Elizabeth, 220
Player, The (film), 141, 191
Plutarch, 168
Political campaigns, 48–51
    See also Presidential candidates
Pollution, 125–127, 134–135
    See also environmental issues
Poor populace, 12, 24, 71, 173–178
    affordable health care and, 95–97,
        98–101, 106–109
    antipoverty policies and, 18–19
    Friedman's theories of, 79,
        80–82
    inefficient policies and, 133–136
    money distribution to, 16–19, 60,
        114
Portfolio managers, 148–151
Postlewaite, Andrew, 176
Poverty. *See* Poor populace
Powell, Colin L., 225
Presidential candidates, 48–51,
    217–219, 225–226
Pricing
    for airline travelers, 118–120
    congestion, 113–116
    and marginal cost, 111–112
    varied, 116–117
    See also Cost-benefit theories
Princeton University, 46
Productivity, 54–57

Progressive consumption taxes,
    31–33, 82, 184–186, 190–191
Proposition 13, CA, 66
Psychology, 58–60, 67
    See also Behavioral economics
Public Service Commission, NY,
    114–115
Public services, 66–67
    See also Welfare programs

Quervain, Dominique de, 222

Racial bias, 224–225, 226
RAND Corporation, 17–18
Range Rovers, 189–191
Reagan, Ronald, 31, 44, 145–146
Rebates, 115–116, 128–130, 131–132
Recessions, 33, 211–214
Regulation, 6, 17
Reilly, Donald, 29
Reimbursements, health care,
    108–109
Retirement, 131–132
Revolutions, 168
Rhodes-Kropf, Matthew, 150
Rich populace. *See* Wealthy
    populace
Rickey, Branch, 226
Ridinger, Amber, 15
Roadrunner (Time Warner
    Internet), 161
Robinson, Jackie, 226
Rockefeller Center, 15
Rodrick, Dani, 29, 167
Roosevelt, Franklin Delano, 147
Rowling, J.K., 155, 156, 157
Rumsfeld, Donald, 216
Russell, Bertrand, 171

Sanctions, 42–44
Saturday Night Live, 157
Savings, 71–72, 181–182, 195
    federal budget deficits and,
        166–167

forces that drive, 193–194, 196–198
Schelling, Thomas C., 6, 73, 97
Schiavo, Terry, 96
Scholarships. *See* Financial: aid
Scientific research programs, 102, 103
Self-interests, 2, 35–39
    invisible hand theories and, 74–76, 199
    volunteering and, 44–48
Shank, Deborah, 93–94
Sherman Antitrust Act, 154
Shifting Involvements (Hirschman), 46
Silicon Valley, 174–175
Simons, James, 148–149
Single payer health care system, 99–101, 102–103
Smith, Adam, 44, 74, 133–134, 174, 183, 199
Social Security system, 194, 197
Social unrest, 168
Socialized medicine, 98–99, 100–101
Sociology, 77
Sopranos, The, 156–157
Spectrem Group, 175
Spending
    class warfare and, 169–172
    forces that drive, 65–66, 193–194
    and Galbraith theories, 76–79
    luxury, 77, 78, 179–186, 188–191
    of middle class versus wealthy, 172, 174–178
Spitzer, Eliot, 219
Sports, professional, 224–225
State governments, 101–104
Stein, Herbert, 168
Stephanopoulos, George, 4
Stigler, George J., 85
Stock Market
    eBay shares of, 158–159
    efficiency, 208–211
    getting rich from, 211–214

Strategy of Conflict, The (Schelling), 74
Subjective well-being. *See* Well-being
Subprime mortgage crisis, 205–208
Subsidies, fuel, 138–139
Survey Research Institute, Cornell University, 24, 25 (table)
Sutton, Willie, 27
SUVs, 120–123, 139–142, 189–191
Swidler, Joseph C., 114

Tax cuts, 20–22, 64–66, 166
    of Bush administration, 10–13, 20–22, 30–31, 33–34, 44, 98, 106
    and fuel subsidies, 138–139
    and traffic congestion, 186–188
    of wealthy populace, 10–13, 172
TaxCut (software), 144
Taxes, 9–11, 126–127, 139
    and earned income credit, 81–82
    estate, 22–27
    on gasoline, 19, 127–133, 134–136
    Health care issues and, 102–103
    for health care reimbursement, 109
    of hedge fund managers, 148–149, 150–151
    invisible hand theories and, 134
    marginal costs and, 120–123
    negative, 80–82
    progressive consumption, 31–33, 82, 184–186, 190–191
    of small business owners, 20–22
    for wealthy, 6, 17–18, 148–149
Taylor, Laura O., 88, 89
Teaching. *See* Education
Tech stocks, 208–211
Technologies, cloning, 145–147
Tester, Jon, 81
Texas A&M University, 186–188
"The Spendings Tax as a Wartime Fiscal Measure" (Friedman), 82
Theories, Economic
    of individual choice, 74–76
    of luxury consumption, 77

Theories, Economic *(continued)*
  and modern game theory, 78
  and trickle-down theory, 27–30
Thompson, Christopher, 220–221
Thune, John, 130, 131
Tiebout, Charles M., 102
Time Warner. *See* AOL-
    TimeWarner merger
Tinbergen, Jan, 79
Tjoa, Bill, 89–90
Tourbillion movement, 14–15
Traffic congestion, 186–188
Tragedy of the commons, 149–150
Trickle-Down Theory, 27–30
Truman, Harry, 9
Trust games, 220–222
Tullock, Gordon, 37
TurboTax, 144
Two Income Trap, The (Warren and
    Tyagi), 206
Tyagi, Amelia Warren, 206

Universal health coverage, 27–28,
    30, 33, 94
University of Chicago, 223
Upper class. *See* Wealthy populace
Urban Institute, 26
U.S. News & World Report, 143
Utilities, 112–113
Utility, 53–54

Vickrey, William, 73
Voice cloning, 146–147
Volcker, Paul A., 225
Volunteering, 44–48

Wages, minimum, 18–19
Walker, Francis Amasa, 1
Wall Street, 151, 199–202
Wall Street Journal, 120, 122,
    157–158
Walmart, 93, 94

Warfare, class, 169–172
Warren, Elizabeth, 206
Washington Post, 178
Waste, 14–16, 137
  government, 9, 13, 66–67
  importance of reducing, 5, 7–8,
    138
Wealth of Nations (Smith), 133, 174,
    199
Wealthy populace, 63–64, 114,
    173–178
  becoming, 211–214
  class warfare and, 168–172
  distributing money to poor and,
    16–19
  savings of, 71–72
  spending of, 180–182, 184–186,
    188–191
  and tax cuts, 10–13
  trickle-down theory and, 27–30
Webb, Jim, 81
Websites, 86, 99
Welch, Jack, 159
Welfare programs, 12, 24, 66–67,
    80–82, 166
Well-being, 57–60, 61–64, 67
What Do You Say to a Naked Lady?
    (film), 140
Windfalls, 72
Winner-take-all markets, 143–145,
    155–157, 165
  cloning technologies and, 146–147
  financial aid and, 152–155
  hedge fund managers of, 148–151
  and internet, 159–162
World Bank, 29
WorldCom, 44
Worth (magazine), 220
Wright, David, 167
Writing, 89–92
Writing in the Disciplines (pilot
    program), 90